WHAT ARE THEY SAYING ABOUT JOHN?
(Revised Edition)

What Are They Saying About John?

(Revised Edition)

Gerard S. Sloyan

PAULIST PRESS
NewYork/Mahwah, N.J.

Scripture quotations are the author's own. Any similarity with other scripture translations is unintentional.

Cover design by James Brisson
Book design by Theresa M. Sparacio

Library of Congress Cataloging-in-Publication Data

Sloyan, Gerard Stephen, 1919–
    What are they saying about John? / Gerard S. Sloyan.—Rev. ed.
      p. cm.
    Includes bibliographical references and indexes.
    ISBN 0-8091-4337-2 (alk. paper)
    1. Bible. N.T. John—Criticism, interpretation, etc. I. Title.
BS2615.2.S565 2006
226.5'06—dc22

                                    2005028076

Published by Paulist Press
997 Macarthur Boulevard
Mahwah, New Jersey 07430

www.paulistpress.com

Printed and bound in the
United States of America

Contents

Introduction

Surely this is a foolhardy venture. Scholarly writing on the Gospel according to John is well-nigh boundless. To attempt a report on the output of the last forty years or so reduces its bulk somewhat, as does confining the work largely to that done in English. A service can undoubtedly be rendered by a report such as this to people who notice the appearance of books and articles but do not have the time to read them, or who remember the status of John studies the last time they did them but have been too busy at other matters to engage in an update. A third class of readers knows the text of John but is unfamiliar with the wars that have raged over its purpose, time and place of origin, mode of composition, rhetorical character, and so on. Given the broad range of persons who may consult these pages, the best approach seemed to be a clear expository one with a minimum of technical terms and transliterated Greek. When terms of scholarly shorthand occur (like *eschatology*), which it would be tedious to many to define, the readers who find them new are referred to an unabridged dictionary.

The scope of writings on John, chosen arbitrarily, is the years 1965–2005. A chapter introductory to this period is placed first. One way of proceeding would have been to group books and articles according to subject matter, theme, or general tendency. This requires a gift of synthesis the present writer may not possess. There was another inhibiting factor at work: The technique runs the risk of betraying the scholars thus classified. After writing 380-page books filled with nuance, they can find themselves lumped together in a parenthesis that says "(so, too, Carpenter, Falegname, and Zimmermann)."

The route chosen in the pages that follow may be even more freighted with peril. It tries to convey the essence of long and complex arguments by transmitting sizable segments of them. Even here the digester may make serious errors in catching the main thrust of a book (less likely, an article). Any scholarly author may cry, "Inadequate grasp!" but my hope is that none cries, "Foul!" Judgment on the quality of the writings reported on is largely left to the reader, a clear possibility if enough evidence has been presented. The subject-matter index thus becomes the key to using this book. As to works not reported on, consulting the multiple citations in the works here mentioned can remedy that.

My one regret is that the list of solid *religious* writings based on the Gospel according to John is so brief. Popularizations of scholarship abound,[1] but the dependable writing on this Gospel suitable for contemplation and prayer, public or private, is regrettably small. Perhaps the exegetical labor had to be done first.

1
The Landmark Commentaries

What Are They Saying About John? They are saying any number of things: some wise, some profound; some historical, some theological; some homiletical, some *religionsgeschichtlich,* a genre that at times is neither historical nor religious. And, yes, some are saying religious things about the Fourth Gospel (which is its sequence in most manuscript codices and all modern Bibles). That there is religious writing on John is as it should be, for its final compiler, along with any who may have produced parts of it, thought their product a religious book. Its purpose — indeed its only purpose — was that the hearer of Jesus' signs recorded in this book should have life by it through faith that Jesus is the Christ, the Son of God. Such was the author's declared intent as chapter 20 came to an end (vv. 30–31). The church included John in its canon for no other purpose. It is a book that promises life.

The First Hundred Years — Heracleon to Origen

There should be no need to review the difficulties experienced by "Jn" — as the canonical Gospel shall be designated here, sometimes "FG" for the Fourth Gospel, and its final editor "John" without prejudging its authorship — in gaining acceptance much

1

before AD 175. The interpretation given to it by Gnostics, who found it supportive of their position, was influential. The anonymous late-second-century **Muratorian Canon,** a fragment of 85 lines in bad Latin probably written at Rome, says in lines 9–16 that John wrote at the urging of his fellow disciples and bishops. They were to "tell one another whatever shall be revealed to each of us."[1] To Andrew, one of John's disciples, it was revealed that "John should write down everything in his own name, while all of them should review it." It was thus conceived of as a synthesis of the revelation shared with the Twelve, coming last of the gospels. (The first line of the fragment, however, begins with mention not of Matthew but of Mark, then Luke.) Discovered in 1740 by Lodovico Muratori, the manuscript explicitly rejects several writings as heretical. This may mean that its acceptance of John is an implicit response to certain heretics of Asia Minor who ascribed it to the Gnostic Cerinthus.

Earlier in that century **Papias of Hierapolis** (AD 70?–140?) had indicated in *The Sayings of the Lord Explained* (a lost work in five books) that he knew John's Gospel, as hinted at by Eusebius[2] and testified to by Jerome and other later fathers.[3] **Justin** (d. ca. 165), who calls the gospels "memoirs of the apostles,"[4] seems to have known John's logos doctrine[5] and in one place quotes the Fourth Gospel.[6] He attributes the millenarian teaching of Revelation (20:4–10) to "John, one of the apostles of Christ."[7] **Hippolytus** of Rome (d. 235) makes the same attribution of the two books to John in a work no longer extant, *On the Gospel of John and the Apocalypse,* rebutting Gaius of Rome over the Johannine authorship of Revelation.[8]

Valentinus, whom **St. Irenaeus** describes as an Egyptian, was the founder of a school at Rome in the mid–second century. In his theogonic and cosmogonic speculations he made much of the prologue of Jn (1:1–18) and had a disciple, **Heracleon,** who probably after 150 wrote the first, very detailed commentary on the Gospel. Origen (d. 253 or 254) preserved many fragments of Heracleon's work in his own commentary that disclose the allegorical hermeneutics of the Gnostic thinker. Thus, for example, the Samaritan woman represents the pneumatic elect; Abraham, Moses, and Jacob the demiurge; and her being told by Jesus to call her husband a revelation that, in her husbandless condition, she has a *"plērōma,"* a "husband in the *aiōn*," who is her *syzygos* (the one to whom she is paired).[9] Irenaeus, Clement of Alexandria, and Origen found this type of exegesis contrived, but it continued to be popular in Christian Gnostic circles, casting a shadow on the FG's orthodoxy. Some Christians even rejected Jn as heretical. Valentinus's disciples produced a *Gospel of Truth,* not presumably the same as the Coptic meditation on salvation of the same name from Nag Hammadi, which evidently served as a kind of shadowy counterpart to the FG.

With Irenaeus's acceptance of Jn in his *Five Books against Gnōsis, Falsely So-Called (Adversus Haereses),* there was expressed the first indisputable claim of apostolic authorship: "Lastly John, the disciple of the Lord, who also lay on his breast, himself published the Gospel, while he was staying at Ephesus in Asia."[10]

The differences between Jn and the Synoptics are so marked—chiefly the extended discourses of Jesus in Jn and the little use of biographical incidents in common, apart from the baptism, the miraculous feeding and walking on water, and the passion and risen life narratives—that a way around the problem was arrived at early. **Clement of Alexandria** wrote:

> Last of all John, perceiving that the external facts *(ta sōmatika)* had been made plain in the gospels, being urged by his friends and inspired by the Spirit…composed a spiritual gospel *(pneumatikon…euaggelion).*[11]

Origen echoed this explanation by observing in his *Commentary on John* at 10.4–6 that strict historical accuracy had to be abandoned because of the needs of spiritual truth. Something like this attempt to account for the differences has continued down to our own time with the popular, conventional view that John presumed a knowledge of the Synoptic details in his hearers and proceeded to present it differently for the sake of deeper understanding. Until recently the opinion prevailed in learned circles that Jn is untrustworthy historically because it is so concerned with theology. A discussion went on concurrently as to whether the author of Jn knew the Synoptics or only the materials on which they drew. His use of the Markan order, even to certain small details, and of Lucan data and development in the passion account heightened the debate.

Some John Scholarship of the Years before World War II: Hoskyns

Any report on "what they are saying about John" needs a starting point, probably best arrived at by "what they *were* saying." For that, an account of certain landmark books produced between 1940 and forty years ago seems to be in order. Those will include the commentaries of **Hoskyns** and **Davey,**[12] Bultmann,[13] Barrett,[14] the two thematic explorations of Dodd,[15] and finally the commentaries of Schnackenburg[16] and Brown.[17] Any number of other commentaries likewise appeared in that period or shortly thereafter, notably those of **Braun,**[18] **Lindars,**[19] and **Haenchen,**[20] but they will not be summarized here. Readers of this book can profitably consult **Robert Kysar**'s examination of Johannine scholarship for the period 1955–75 (at this writing out of print), brought up to date in a not so readily accessible bibliographical tool,[21] and before that a 1955 updating of a summary by British scholar **W. F. Howard**.[22]

Sir Edwyn Hoskyns of Cambridge worked on his commentary on Jn for fourteen years. At his death in 1937 he left six completed chapters ready for the press and another seventeen in rough form. These Francis Noel Davey published in a book of 604 pages.[23] Hoskyns seems to have relied most on Adolf Schlatter's commentary of 1930. He takes no position on the authorship of Jn except to assume, more than argue, that the same person wrote the Johannine epistles, probably somewhere in Syria. For Hoskyns the ultimate authority underlying the Johannine writings was theological. They were addressed to people who had a great deal of miscellaneous information about the Lord's life ("episodic" is his description of the Synoptic Gospels, documents that he does not think the author of the FG possessed). John saw that the tradition had an underlying meaning, "peering out of it at every point, a meaning which is 'beyond history,' and which alone makes sense of history. To disclose this underlying history of the tradition he wrote his gospel."[24] The Gospel was written for Christians and contained a polemic against Jews but was not directed against Ebionites, Gnostics, or any other group. The author wants his hearers to go behind him and the church to the apostles, and behind them to the visible, historical Jesus. Behind Jesus lies the glory of the Son of God, the Word. But Jn and the church and Jesus are ultimately meant to rest in God, who was self-manifested— given as an epiphany to the world—in this Son.

The matrix of the Gospel, with its constant reference to the Hebrew scriptures and Palestinian geography, was Jewish, not Christian or Mandean-Gnostic. Hoskyns knew an article of Rudolf Bultmann from 1925, prompted by the researches of Orientalist M. Lidzbarski, claiming that a Gnostic redeemer myth with the Baptist at its center underlay the Johannine prologue. This he rejected along with the primary influence of Hellenic thought on the Gospel, although "the Evangelist may have recognized that the Christian teaching concerning the Word of God had further implications for Greeks familiar with the Stoic conception of the divine Logos or Person."[25] Hoskyns entertains no scruple about speaking of the Jews' "national rejection of Christ" (p. 273; sometimes "the Jewish authorities"), hence the Jews as the targets of the FG without further nuance.

The commentary that follows each pericope of the Gospel in the Revised Version (1881) makes extensive use of philological arguments from the critical readings of the text that Hoskyns defends, and the church fathers. The erudition of the part labeled "Commentary" is impressive. The reflections that immediately follow the Bible text are theological and at times meditative in the best homiletical style. There are numerous "Detached Notes" throughout, for example, the one on Jn 1:13 that provides all the arguments for and against a singular rather than a plural reading, "who was born not of bloods," and so on, making it not believers born of God but Jesus virginally born of Mary. Here Hoskyns simply provides the (weak) textual evidence and surprisingly strong patristic support of the idea, leaving the reader to conclude wrongly that the evidence against the plural reading (the blood of Joseph and Mary as the deduction) was overwhelming. The subsequent consensus goes against Hoskyns on textual grounds, seeing in the threefold denial (despite the "bloods") an affirmation of Jesus' childhood of God by divine initiative through faith. While the observations on the individual vignettes and discourses of Jesus are fraught with learned detail, Hoskyns ventures that the encounter of the church with the Spirit through the person of Jesus is the overarching theme for the whole Gospel. The Synoptic use of traditional eschatological terms has become, "in an evolution of perception," a conscious theological language of the Spirit. The "urgent, final impact of God upon the world," which eschatology is concerned to proclaim, "is now expressed as theology," a theology inherent in the Markan reminiscences of a generation before.[26] As to the historical character of the Gospel, Hoskyns assumes that everything somehow happened in Jesus' life as reported in the FG, while acknowledging the impossibility of distinguishing history from interpretation. His introduction allows the possibility that historical occurrences may be given a symbolic value in Jn, but this is not much adverted to in his subsequent exegeses. The relation of the FG to the earlier tradition of the Synoptics and before absorbs most of his energies.

The Influential Work of Bultmann

Rudolf Bultmann altered the course of Johannine studies radically in a book published while Germany was at war (1941). Hoskyns's work had been produced between World War I and the Great Depression but its impact, like Bultmann's, was not felt until after World War II. Bultmann's *The Gospel of John* leaps immediately into seventy pages of commentary on the book's first eighteen verses, without an introduction. There the reader is introduced to the Marburg scholar's two main convictions: that a cultic community hymn based on a pre-Christian Gnostic redeemer myth underlies the prologue (1:1–18), part of a collection of Gnostic "revelation discourses" that are the basis of the Jesus discourses in the Gospel,[27] and that the FG should be read existentially as promising man *(Mensch)* freedom from death, "the fate that makes existence sheerly unintelligible."[28] Jesus' prime function as the Son is to be the Revealer of God. God's glory *(doxa)* is manifested in history in the Word become flesh, a Word that brings the knowledge of God that Jesus both speaks and himself *is*.[29]

Bultmann does not believe that the evangelist is committed to the metaphysical dualism between matter and spirit that he finds in his Gnostic source. The "evangelist" designates the penultimate writer who framed a gospel that the "editor" later presented to the church. The spirit-matter dualism concept of Gnosticism, like that of the preexistence of souls and other aspects of the myth, is edited out. For Bultmann, Jesus is a human figure "pure and simple," the revealer of the glory of God who is uniquely God's Son. Jesus as Logos is a salvific intermediary between God and the world in the same way that the Gnostic Wisdom is, on whom that late biblical equivalent of Torah draws. Personified Wisdom, in Bultmann's view, is drawn from pagan myth.

None of the arguments leveled against Bultmann, which maintain that all the "Gnostic influences" on Jn he cites were post-Johannine (among them the Odes of Solomon, the letters of Ignatius, the Christian Gnostic corpus, and the Hermetic and

Mandean literatures), dislodged his conviction that a well-formulated revealer-redeemer myth lay behind the Gospel we have in hand. The "revelation-discourses source" that drew on the myth, produced in poetic-sounding Aramaic, was one major building block of the Gospel. The other was the "signs source," a collection of Synoptic-like miracle stories distinct from those of the Synoptic traditions. For narrative elements in stories such as those of Nicodemus, the Samaritan woman, and the man blind from birth, the evangelist acted creatively, drawing on "miscellaneous sources": snatches of reminiscence, parables of Jesus, and the like. The fourth source posited is a "passion and risen-life source" that came to the evangelist in semitized Greek.

The Way the Evangelist Used His Four Sources

Bultmann's major project, perhaps, was to identify the evangelist as the weaver of his sources into a continuous narrative to which an editor gave final shape. This was done by assuming that the materials that lay behind the Gospel were each of them perfectly consistent in vocabulary and style. Any abrupt transitions, therefore, in the present Gospel or any passages uncharacteristic of the evangelist's editorial style signal the insertion of material from a source. Put in reverse, the characteristics of each source are so distinctive that each of the sources can be separated out. Thus, the "incongruities in the relationship of a passage to its context are the basic means of detecting the sources, the evangelist, and the redactor [editor] (context criticism)."[30]

To choose an example: Bultmann finds it clear that Jn 1:22–24 is an insertion by the editor into the text of the evangelist. It is the evangelist's idea that the Baptist is but a witness to Jesus, who is a prophet and the Christ.[31] The three verses break the continuity between vv. 21 and 25 of the source because the Baptist's denials of who he is (vv. 20–21) are not logically followed by the characterization of him in vv. 22–24. Hence, an ecclesiastical editor who knew the traditional use of Is 40:3 must have inserted it at this point. Further, v. 26 should clearly be followed by v. 31 because, linked together by the verb *know*, they answer the question put in v. 25, "If you are not the Messiah, nor Elijah, nor the Prophet, why do you baptize?"

> V. 27 is again an additional comment from the Synoptic tradition (Mk 1.7 par.); v. 28 on the other hand is the original conclusion of the section[1] [1 cp. the conclusions 6:59; 8:20; 12:36] and originally came after v. 34. Vv. 29–30 are connected with v. 28. The misplacing of vv. 28–30 can be attributed only to the disorder of the text which the editor had before him.[32]

The section ends with the "original text of the Gospel" in Greek, with appropriate verse numbers, in the following sequence: 1:1, 20, 21, 25, 26, 31, 33, 34, 28, and "there follow vv. 29–30."[33] Something similar is done with the "original" order of chs. 4–6 (4, 6, 5)[34] and 13–17 ("13.1–30 records Jesus' last meal with his disciples; 17.1–26 gives us the farewell prayer; 13.31–35; 15.1–16.33; 13.36–14.31 contain the farewell discourses and conversations").[35]

It would be a mistake to think that Bultmann's theory of the ingenious and complex composition of the Gospel in its present form was his chief contribution to its study. It is true that he solved many problems posed by the aporias (awkward transitions) that abound in Jn. But the theory of a signs source that he based on a 1922 article of A. Faure in *ZNW*[36] is his contribution that remains. His theory that the evangelist likewise drew on a discourses source has largely yielded to one that sees the evangelist himself as the composer of Jesus' discourses. Kysar presents in schematic form the contents that five later authors assign to the signs source. Two of them, Teeple and Fortna, think that a passion or passion-resurrection source was a part of it.[37]

The Consensus of the 1980s on Bultmann's Composition Theory

Important as Bultmann's work on sources has been to Johannine scholarship, it has led to a verdict of "not proven" with respect to any but a signs source. His inability to convince large numbers that the evangelist possessed a Gnostic redeemer myth that he reworked, placing Jesus at the center, derived as much from the intricacy of the editorial process he assumed as from doubts that such a pre-Christian myth existed. In his apodicticism lay his failure, his certitude that a herald of the gospel would so deliver himself over to a pagan literary composition.

Where Bultmann succeeded was in identifying the evangelist's theological project. This was, first, in chs. 3–12 to portray the revelation of God's glory to the world in Jesus—the struggle between light and darkness hinted at in 1:5, 9–11. The result of this epiphany was *krisis* in the sense of both "judgment" and "division." Chapters 13–20 portray the revelation of the "glory" to believers, or the victory of the light, thereby illustrating 1:12–18.[38]

The final editor's ecclesial concern with the sacraments of baptism and Eucharist, which Bultmann categorizes as Hellenist in origin and trivial relative to the Gospel's message of belief in the Son, is another a priori of the Marburger, like that of the redeemer myth.

His formidable knowledge of pagan Greek and Christian sectarian writings commands respect, although in rabbinic matters he is often confined to what Strack-Billerbeck's anthology tells him. His command of the exegetical literature had no parallel in Johannine scholarship up to his time. This, plus his firm grasp on the overall design of the evangelist, continues to make his commentary worth consulting before anything more recent is looked at. His individualist interpretations of a message directed at a believing *people* and his insensitivity to the Jewish character of Christianity, as if that aspect were somehow related to Jn's *Ioudaioi*, can be looked past. Bultmann has many insightful things to say about light and darkness in Jn, faith and unbelief, the intimate relation between the Father and the Son, and of both to those who believe in him.

The English Tradition in Johannine Studies, Continued

C. K. Barrett reports in the preface to the second edition of his *The Gospel according to St. John* that it was rejected from a series for its length and detail but rescued for the publisher SPCK by the good offices of F. N. Davey.[39] Seeing it as a "juvenile work" twenty-three years later, he acknowledges he has learned much from later commentators but, by his own account, has adopted few new positions. Barrett thinks that Mk is a source for Jn and that Lk probably is too in a smaller degree; Jn deliberately reworked sayings and incidents from the two in light of his overall purpose. This was to set forth the traditional faith in a new idiom, to strengthen those unsettled by winds of Gnostic doctrine, to win new converts, and to provide a more adequate exposition of the faith itself.[40] Qumrân does not unlock much in Jn, nor can the historical traditions discernible in Jn be readily disentangled from the interpretive comments. For Barrett a discourse source is even less provable than a signs source, and a Jerusalem source is not likely at all. The Johannine passion story is an edited version of the Markan into which Jn has introduced some fresh material. Theories of displacement and subsequent redaction create as many problems as they solve. It is doubtful, finally, whether Q ever existed.

John knew the Septuagint, the Hebrew Bible, apocalyptic Judaism and rabbinic exegesis, popular Platonic-Stoic teaching, and the light/life material that would emerge in the 2nd–4th c. *Hermetica*. Barrett finds in Philo the best witness to pre-Christian Gnosis, which "plays some part in the make-up of Johannine thought."[41] John fused Jewish and Hellenist elements into "a unitary presentation of the universal significance of Jesus,"[42] laying both Jewish thought and Greek metaphysics under tribute in his

Christology. Whereas the Synoptics "simply view Jesus in the light of the eschatological crisis which he precipitated...John releases himself from a purely apocalyptic interpretation of Jesus, while he continues to use eschatological language (though not exclusively)."[43] He presents Jesus as the first creator and the final judge, the ultimate truth both of God and of humanity, the image of God and the archetype of humanity, an ontological mediator between God and man. Jesus himself is the bearer of the Spirit; he also bestows the Spirit, the power at work in the church's mission and the source of its authority. The Spirit works by revealing the truth and relating the church positively to the truth upon which it stands. By so doing, this Spirit reacts negatively upon the world, which is judged.[44]

Barrett sees no opposition between "the disciple whom Jesus loved" (13:23; 19:26f.; 20:2; 21:7, 20) and the Twelve, to whom he probably belonged. For the University of Durham scholar, John the son of Zebedee, who was not the evangelist, was probably that beloved disciple. He migrated to Ephesus and died there, leaving behind an unnamed follower who composed chs. 1–20. Another disciple of John wrote the Apocalypse from John's authentic works. Probably two disciples wrote 1 Jn and 2 and 3 Jn. The author of Jn 21 sought to establish the association of Peter and the beloved disciple as partners, neither taking precedence. Peter is the head of the evangelistic and pastoral work of the church, but the beloved disciple is the guarantor of its tradition regarding Jesus.[45]

Perhaps the strongest feature of the commentary, which may also be its enduring worth, is its careful attention to the manuscript witness or state of the text. Second in importance to these attempts to establish the product of the final redactor is Barrett's grammatical concern. Arguing both on his own and from authority, he debates constantly the renderings that ambiguities in the Greek will admit and votes on how to settle them. The same is true of John's style on the basis of word count, grammatical construction, and parallel usages from the time. The notes on individual verses tend to satisfy in the wealth of background they provide.

Barrett adopts the view that "when all has been reviewed it is difficult to resist the impression that the Palestinian material has been disposed according to the demands of a dominant non-Jewish partner."[46] Studies of the last fifty years have concluded that not everything Jewish in the first century was Palestinian and that Palestine was not free of weighty Hellenist influence. Barrett may be the last of a long line of Johannine scholars to think that in Jn the non-Jewish partner dominated.

A Congregationalist Scholar Follows upon a Methodist

C. H. Dodd's *The Interpretation of the Fourth Gospel* is too early for adequate treatment within this survey.[47] Its importance lay in its exploration of the background of the Fourth Gospel—which needed an inquiry that was not antecedently committed as Bultmann's was. Dodd coupled his research into possible literary and religious influences with a presentation of twelve leading ideas in Jn and a breakdown of its argument and structure. The Hermetic corpus of Greek writings from Egypt, in which Poimandres (a "Shepherd") is the divine revealer, shows how important the pagans considered knowledge of God was to salvation and how widespread the conception was of the deity as life and light. The Gnostic systems exposed by Irenaeus and Hippolytus, who were later to be sustained in their general accuracy by the Nag Hammadi finds of 1945 in Upper Egypt, are seen as derived from Oriental mythology more than Hellenic or Hebraic origins. Dodd showed that the formulation of a Gnostic myth as complete in the pre-Christian period remains as much a matter of speculation as when Reitzenstein first posited it. The two books of the Mandeans, moreover (*Manda d'Hayye* = "Knowledge of Life"), a Gnostic offshoot, are shown to go back no further than AD 700, whatever the age of their claim that John the Baptist was their founder. Lidzbarski's theory, seized upon by Reitzenstein and Bultmann, that an Iranian redemption myth underlay the religion of followers of the Baptist (see Acts 18:24 — 19:7), from which Christianity derived, is shown to be highly doubtful, not least because the Christian heresiologists are silent about the Mandeans from the first century to the eighth.

Dodd's thematic study of Johannine symbolism under leading ideas such as eternal life, knowledge of God, truth, spirit, and logos, and light, glory, and judgment was very helpful to readers confined to English-language scholarship six decades ago. This was especially true because it never left biblical or pseudepigraphic sources aside while paying attention to Philonic and other Hellenic developments. Dodd's synthesis shed light on the rich religious vocabulary available to John without the evangelist's having to draw directly on this or that "source." Well past the midpoint of the book the Gospel begins to be dealt with chapter by chapter, under the threefold heading The Proem (1:1–18 prologue and 10–51 testimony), The Book of Signs (chs. 2–12), and The Book of the Passion (chs. 13–20 with ch. 21 as a postscript). The Book of Signs is divided into seven episodes, not all of them with a miracle at the core, and an epilogue. They are: The New Beginning, 2:1 — 4:42; The Life Giving Word, 4:46 — 5:47; Bread of Life, 6; Light and Life: Manifestation and Rejection, 7–8; Judgment by the Light, 9:1 — 10:21 with appendix, 10:22–39; The Victory of Life over Death, 11:1–53; Life through Death: The Meaning of the Cross, 12:1–36; and, as a postscript to these eleven chapters, 12:37–50. The chief insight of this first book of Dodd's is that provided by chs. 2–4, where the inauguration of a new order of life in the enfleshed Word is examined in a succession of symbols of newness: new wine, new worship, new birth, a new bridegroom, new life-giving water, a new people where there had been two, and new life—all enclosed by a first sign (2:11) and a second (4:54).

Dodd's second volume, *Historical Tradition in the Fourth Gospel,* was published a decade later.[48] The author describes it as an expansion of the Appendix to the earlier work, "Some

Considerations upon the Historical Aspect of the Fourth Gospel."[49] There he had written:

> The use of freely composed speeches to elucidate the significance of events does not in itself impugn the historical character of the narrative in the Fourth Gospel, any more than in Thucydides or Tacitus. There is however good reason to suspect that in some cases and in some respects the narratives which provide the setting for such speeches may have been moulded by the ideas which they are made to illustrate.[50]

Maintaining as established by form criticism that the narratives of the first three gospels have been thus molded, Dodd holds that there is no more reason to deny a historical character to the FG than to attribute a large measure of historicity to the Synoptics. The topographical references in Jn (Sychar, Ephraim, Bethany beyond Jordan, and six others) can scarcely have been inserted, he thinks, for symbolic reasons. But when, in this second volume, he meticulously analyzes the Johannine passages most closely related to the Synoptic materials, he concludes that Jn (at least in 13:16; 12:25; 13:20; 20:23) "is not dependent on the Synoptic Gospels, but is transmitting independently a special form of the common oral tradition."[51] His conclusion, which is based on the accumulation of probabilities, is that

> behind the Fourth Gospel lies an ancient tradition independent of the other gospels, and meriting serious consideration as a contribution to our knowledge of the historical facts concerning Jesus Christ....All through I have assumed that the tradition we are trying to track down was oral...[although] written sources may have intervened between the strictly oral tradition and our Fourth Gospel.[52]

Dodd thinks it may be said of this precanonical tradition that it shows contact with an Aramaic tradition ("The evangelist himself was probably a speaker of Aramaic"), that it appears "to point to a

Jewish (Jewish-Christian) setting," and that it retains allusions to well-attested Jewish beliefs and has points of contact with Jewish tradition. In summary, "the basic tradition…on which the evangelist is working was shaped (it appears) in a Jewish-Christian environment still in touch with the synagogue, in Palestine, at a relatively early date, at any rate before the rebellion of A.D. 66.…Yet there are in places signs of development either at a later date or outside Palestine, or both."[53] To examine those conclusions carefully is to see that the Jewishness of the Gospel is taken as a sign of proximity to the actual events narrated, that "the tradition" is basically a matter of historicity, and that a leap has been made from the text of Jn and the Synoptics back to a preliterary, oral tradition—two distinct traditions, in fact—on which the first written collections of sayings and stories were based.

John's Gospel as a Witness to the Events of History

Whatever else may be said of Dodd's *Historical Tradition,* he is to be thanked for his exhaustive analysis of Johannine passages where the wording is similar to that of any of the Synoptics and where the underlying ideas are related, whether the relationship be close or tenuous. He does this by starting with the passion narrative under seven headings because there the likenesses are closest. Summing up after 150 pages of sifting the similarities, he concludes that there is no sufficient evidence to prove a literary dependence of the Gospel of John on the others in this part of the Gospel. "On the contrary there is cumulative evidence that the Johannine version represents (subject to some measure of 'writing up' by the evangelist) an independent strain of the common oral tradition, differing from the strains of tradition underlying Mark (Matthew) and Luke, though controlled by the same general *schema.*"[54] Interestingly, Dodd takes the exchange between Jesus and Pilate (Jn 18:28—19:16) as evidence of Jn's boldness, as it represents Jesus' condemnation to be the result of a clash between his claims and those of Caesar. Dodd even permits himself to wonder if "We have no king but Caesar" was a profession of Jewish loyalty at the place where the Gospel was written, as contrasted with a less than full allegiance by the followers of Jesus in the same locality. He writes: "I could much more easily believe that the Synoptists have reduced the political element in the tradition that had come down to them."[55] Granting the likelihood of "a certain amount of elaboration" in the two hearings before Pilate in camera, Dodd thinks that "it remains probable that the tradition upon which this elaboration was based...may well have been in some respects more fully informed [than Mark's]."[56]

Dealing with the ministry of Jesus as the second narrative portion of Jn by proceeding backward from the passion, and the story of the Baptist and the first disciples as the third portion, historical tradition concludes that John, Mark, and Luke used separate strands of tradition for the anointing stories,[57] and that the healing stories of Jn had no common nucleus with those of the Synoptics.[58] A traditional narrative underlies Jn's account of the resuscitation of Lazarus, which has been shaped in the course of Christian preaching and teaching. John has "remoulded [it] to convey his own special message,"[59] even as Mk has done with his distinct healing and resuscitation traditions. The tradition on the Baptist in Jn "included very primitive material, but before it reached our evangelist it had undergone development in the environment indicated (viz., one in which Christians claimed the Baptist as the first 'confessor' of Jesus, made long before the gospel was written)."[60] Dodd finds seven sayings of Jesus that are parabolic in form (7:24; 16:21; 11:9–10; 8:35; 10:1–5; 3:29; 5:19–20a). "Yet in no case is there the remotest likelihood of derivation from Synoptic sources."[61] And so the whole work concludes that in every instance cited or explored Jn is found to have reached back to "a very early form of tradition indeed...making it the point of departure for his profound theological reinterpretation."[62] But that traditional source is never the one that is drawn on by the Synoptics.

The chief impression left by the meticulous and at times tedious word study of this book is that the author is unwilling to depart from the earlier conventional wisdom that an evangelist was above all an editor of received traditions.[63] When one of them—apart from Mt's obvious editing of Mk's and Lk's less evident efforts, and the incorporation of Q sayings by Lk and Mt— engages in the pure genius of authorship, it is grudgingly acknowledged as a brief patch of elaboration or composition. A second absentee from the discussion is the lively role played by orality in first-century composition.[64] The evangelists are assumed to have been seated in studies surrounded by the LXX, the Masoretic Text, several targums, and numerous scraps of written gospel tradition to which the oral had been reduced. But this is an imposition of twentieth-century scholarly methods on the first century.[65] A writer like the evangelist John would have had endless passages of the Bible committed to memory, both exactly and inexactly. He would have known how he had been accustomed to proclaim the gospel over decades without being able to cite all the ways in which traditions had come to him. Faced with this writing challenge, the evangelist, as distinct from the final editor, might have sought out some written sources he had not consulted in years—like anyone in the literary game. Of the heavy dependence of any ancient writer on heard, memorized, and spoken transmission as contrasted with the careful copying out of written sources, there is no clue in Dodd.

A U.S. Scholar Enters the Lists

Raymond E. Brown's *The Gospel according to John* was published in two volumes, in 1966 and 1970, as indicated above (see n. 17). Numerous section references to the second volume as well as numbered appendixes appeared in the first, indicating that the whole work already existed in some, if not final, form. The two Jn volumes are of 538 and 670 pages, the first preceded by an introduction that runs to 145 pages. Apart from its exhaustive reference to Johannine literature (well beyond that in English and German) and its balanced judgments, the commentary recommends itself for its clarity of exposition and pattern of organization. The introduction in ten numbered parts deals with subjects such as the unity and composition of the Fourth Gospel, the tradition behind it, proposed influences on its religious thought, the destination and purpose of the Gospel, and the identity of the author and its place of composition. An eleventh part is a general selective bibliography of twenty-eight works that were actually used, none older than 1928 besides Loisy and Schürer. As one reaches the commentary proper (forty-five sections in the first volume, thirty-eight in the second), one finds first the translation of a pericope, then notes that are chiefly observations on words and phrases, often raising questions to be resolved in the third part, headed "Comment." This is frequently divided into "General" and "Specific" (sometimes "Detailed"), but not in the case of shorter pericopes such as 1:29–34 (dealt with in section 3) or the four pericopes and their comments into which 6:1–34 is broken. The Greek and Hebrew are transliterated into English, something Dodd did not do (nor with Syriac!). Bibliographies are provided at the end of each section, and outlines of what to expect in the Gospel precede them. These pedagogic helps, glossaries in the appendixes, and charts comparing Jn with the Synoptics (as in the multiplication of the loaves and the Barabbas incident) make this commentary a very usable tool indeed.

A Theory of Composition That Has Come to Prevail

A feature found in the introduction that has proved durable over the last forty-plus years is Brown's theory of the five stages of Jn's composition, two preliterary and three in its written form. These are: (1) a collection of traditional materials containing the words and works of Jesus, independent in origin from the Synoptic tradition(s); (2) oral preaching and teaching over several decades that molded the tradition in the form and style that came to characterize the FG: short dramas worked up around Jesus' miracles (including the now familiar Johannine misunderstandings and ironies); lengthy discourses devised by members of a school that had one principal preacher; toward the end of this second stage, written forms of what was preached and taught; (3) the material from stage 2 woven into the first edition of a consecutive gospel, the work of a master teacher and theologian; (4) a second edition (and possibly more) by this same evangelist to meet the objections or difficulties of groups such as followers of the Baptist, and believers in Jesus associated with the synagogue; (5) a final editing or redaction not always easily distinguishable from stage 4, most likely by a disciple of the evangelist and part of his school: chs. 15–17 added to Jesus' supper discourse with 16:4–33 a variant duplicate of ch. 15, likewise the Lazarus story (chs. 11 and 12 possibly added at stages 4 or 5), an insertion that could have caused the shift of the cleansing of the Temple to ch. 2; the eucharistic words of Jesus at the supper placed in ch. 6, thus associating the two events with a different Passover from the final one in stage 4. In all, the final redactor, like the evangelist in his second edition, used additional materials developed within the Johannine school.

Brown had called ch. 21 an epilogue in his early outline and identifies it in his second volume as the work of the redactor of chs. 1–20 or perhaps another. This editor, who is not the evangelist and who has more ancient material to add, is certainly not Bultmann's Ecclesiastical Redactor, whose outlook on church and sacraments is thought to be quite foreign to that of the evangelist.[66]

Brown gives his reasons for thinking that the Gospel in its present form was written between 80 and 110, probably toward 100 and in Ephesus (where Revelation was the more primitive product of the Johannine school) rather than Alexandria or Antioch. As to authorship, he finds it hard to argue against the unanimous external testimony that it was the work of John, son of Zebedee. He also thinks John the best candidate for "the disciple whom Jesus loved" (over Lazarus, John Mark, or an unknown disciple, surely not one other than a member of the Synoptics' Twelve). On internal evidence, there is the attribution of the gospel tradition to an eyewitness disciple in 19:35; cf. 21:24, which attributes testimony to "these things" (ch. 21? the whole Gospel?) to the disciple whom Jesus loved of v. 20. He is obviously the same person as the one at the foot of the cross in 19:26 but also distinguished from the "we" of 21:24 who wrote ch. 21. There are six references in all to the disciple whom Jesus loved, designated BD by Brown for "beloved disciple": 13:23–26; 19:25–27; 20:2–10; 21:7, 21–23 (with reference back to 13:23–26); 21:24 ("this same disciple" as "witness for these things"). Once, "another disciple…known to the high priest" is spoken of with Peter (18:15–16) while "the one Jesus loved" of 21:2–10 is also called "the other disciple." Brown thinks it plausible that "an (the) other disciple" is this person's self-designation while his status as beloved of Jesus is the work of his own followers. No one seems to Brown more likely than the disciple John to be the one who has preserved his memories of Jesus and was closely associated with Peter. The son of Zebedee could well have been Jesus' first cousin, son of Salome, Jesus' mother's sister (see the note on 19:25).

Brown faces the formidable difficulties raised against his position by stating initially that almost every account of the composition from the patristic period associates others with John. The apostle cannot have been the final redactor of stage 5 because the "we" of 21:24 is distinct from the BD, who was also probably dead when the chapter was written (see vv. 22–23). But he could have been and "probably [was] the source of the historical tradition behind the Fourth Gospel."[67] More than the source, in his preaching he "would necessarily have had to adapt to his audience the tradition of which he was a living witness."[68] So much for stage 1, but was he responsible for stages 2 through 4? For these he provided guidance and encouragement, especially to the "*one principal disciple* whose transition of the historical material received

from John was marked with dramatic genius and profound theological insight, and it is the preaching and teaching of this disciple
that gave shape to the stories and discourses now found in the
Fourth Gospel."[69] Brown gives this disciple-evangelist no name
but notes that some may be attracted by the hypothesis of John the
Presbyter, named by Papias ca. 130.

Some Further Positions of Brown

While acknowledging that Jn's revelatory discourses are not
Greek poetry or Semitic, in Burney's back-translation into Aramaic, Brown describes his search for the format into which he set
these discourses in English translation. Bultmann had done the
same arranging of lines in Greek, and Donatien Mollat in French
for *La Bible de Jérusalem,* but the problems are obviously different in each language. Consulting those three and the earlier
attempt of Gächter, Brown found the principles of division
entirely flexible, and hence proceeded to render the quasi-poetic
prose ("solemn [but] far from lyrical…[a repetition achieving]
monotonous grandeur") into sense lines in ordinary English
resembling the nonliterary Greek.

In treating the opening verses of Jn (1:1–18), Brown takes
them to be a Christ hymn composed in the Johannine church. He
compares it to the hymns of Phil 2:6–11, Col 1:15–20, and 1 Tim
3:16 and finds them not dissimilar. Opting for the verses that constituted the original hymn is not easy; among the eight authors
whose choices he cites, no two make the same choice. Brown
votes, tentatively, for four strophes composed of vv. 1–2, 3–5,
10–12b, and 14, 15, a reconstruction unlike any of the other eight.
An editor, he thinks, has inserted the prose account about the
preaching of John into the poem (vv. 6–9, 12c–14, 16), but he
finds "interesting" the suggestion of Boismard and others that the
Gospel originally began with "There was sent by God a man

named John" (as in the Samson narrative of Judges), into which the hymn was intercalated.

As to the Word of the prologue, it is a divine communication to humanity in which the messenger himself is the message. The opening words of Genesis repeated here "are peculiarly fitting to open the account of what God has said and done in the new dispensation."[70] The career of the Word in the world has empowered people to become God's children (v. 12), something heretofore unachievable (in the sense of their being begotten from above by the Spirit of Jesus, 3:15). The rejection of the Word by men in v. 10 ("his own people," in v. 11) has no anti-Jewish overtones for Brown, being quite like the human rejection of Wisdom in Enoch 42:2: "Wisdom came to make her dwelling among human offspring and found no dwelling place." Similarly, "the Jews" is used interchangeably with the chief priests and the Pharisees as "almost a technical title for *the religious authorities, particularly those in Jerusalem, who are hostile to Jesus.*"[71] "Israel" is Jn's favorable term, "the Jews" often—although not always—his unfavorable term (chs. 11–12 constitute an exception, where he holds it means Judeans). Brown thinks that by the time the FG was written in its final form, the Jews who believed in Jesus would no longer have been designated as Jews, nor does the law any longer affect them.[72]

As part of this there is his conviction, held by W. D. Davies and others, that the Eighteen Benedictions were reformulated ca. 85 so that the twelfth "was a curse on the *minim* or heretics, primarily Jewish-Christian."[73] Recited publicly, it was thus a trap calculated to make believers in Jesus curse themselves, much like Edward Everett Hale's fictitious Philip Nolan choking on the recitation of Scott's *Innominatus* on shipboard. Important to this outlook is the supposition that the seemingly technical term *aposynágōgos (-oi)* of 9:22, 12:42, and 16:2 came closest in meaning to total ejection from Israel toward the end of the first century.[74] The separation of Christians from Jews as a distinct religious community is thus taken for granted within sixty years after the resurrection, on the further assumption that the decree of the academy at Yavneh was acted upon throughout the Mediterranean Jewish world.

As Brown proceeds through an exhaustive interpretation of the minidramas and discourses that go to make up Jn, he expounds fully the critical theories with which he cannot agree. This he does so evenhandedly that often, after he has presented three or four opinions, the reader cannot tell where he will come out. Unlike many exegetes, he presents the views of church fathers of the East and West, which often prove surprisingly modern. The Catholic scholarship of Europe likewise gets a hearing it has not received in German- and British-dominated scholarship. If being "conservative" means taking seriously positions sanctioned by long-standing acceptance, Brown is conservative. He is, at the same time, occasionally as radical as any critic.[75] One thing the reader can count on regularly is his lack of enthusiasm for source criticism, understood as confidently assigning pericopes to written sources and not hesitating to identify their beginning or end, even if it should occur in midverse. He simply does not think the Gospel came into existence by that careful stitching process. It was, rather, a compilation from a large Johannine pool, the work of a "school" that seemed to have as its primary conviction that nothing of the developed historical tradition should be lost. Displacements, awkward "seams," and the like did not bother the final redactor(s) so long as, in some fashion, it was all *there.*

Like Bultmann, Brown is always worth consulting, even by those who are predisposed to find one right and the other wrong. Before these two vote on a phrase, a passage, or the Gospel's whole drift, they give a hearing to massive amounts of evidence.

A Magisterial Work Appearing Shortly after Brown's

With **Rudolf Schnackenburg,** a Catholic professor at Würzburg, it is much the same as with Bultmann and Brown. The first volume of his commentary was published at the same time as Brown's and was completed over a ten-year period.[76] He draws on a wide range of northern European and British scholarship and is more venturesome than Brown in his reconstructions of the present text of Jn. He holds that chs. 5 and 6 originally occurred in reverse order, 7:15–24 coming after 5:47.[77] This sequence keeps Jesus in Galilee for the miracle of the loaves, ch. 6 following immediately on ch. 4, then presents a Sabbath healing in Jerusalem (5:8) that triggers the clash that continues with growing intensity throughout the feast of Tabernacles. Schnackenburg like Brown supposes that the series of farewell discourses in chs. 15–17, all by the same author, were inserted after 14:31 by later editors who left the finality of that verse ("Come, then. Let us be on our way") intact. There are other displacements he identifies but cannot account for quite so readily, like 3:31–36 and 12:44–50. The first is clearly not an utterance of the baptizing prophet John, both because of its contents and because the evangelist, "contrary to a fairly widespread opinion, always marks off Jesus' discourses clearly."[78] Placing the segment of discourse after 3:21 would solve one problem but create others. As to the second pericope, 12:44–50, it is clearly anticlimactic to the final reflections contained in vv. 37–43 but is not easily situated in its proper place.

Schnackenburg sees in Jn a writer who supposes in his readers a knowledge of several matters in the Synoptic tradition but not known to them from it. Like Brown, he posits a substratum or early stage of the Johannine tradition that may be contemporaneous with the Synoptic tradition. Jn's main interest is clear: "to delineate boldly the majestic figure of the eschatological bringer of revelation and salvation, to display the radiant glory of the Logos as he lives on earth and dwells among us, to disclose the ever-present significance of the saving events which lie in the past."[79]

Whoever "the evangelist" or basic author of Jn was, for Schnackenburg he did not write under Gnostic influences of the kind that surface in the Nag Hammadi texts or Odes of Solomon. Neither must the idea that a simple Galilean fisherman could not have risen to the spiritual heights of the Fourth Gospel be accepted without question. The content, language, and thought of Jn point to a Hellenistic disciple of the apostle who committed it to writing, probably as the member of a school or evangelizing company, with the possible mediation of a venerable preacher responsible for the typical Johannine discourses of Jesus. Schnackenburg is sure that the BD was a historical, not a symbolic, figure, but at first cannot come down firmly on the side of his having been the son of Zebedee or any other individual. This does not keep him from maintaining that the ancient apostolic authority behind Jn is Zebedee's son in the early stages of the tradition. Written sources to which Lk and even Mk had access could also have been influential. (Brown, incidentally, does not outlaw the possibility of a Johannine redactor's having known Mk's Gospel.) Schnackenburg's ultimate decision on the BD is that the disciples of the apostle John, including the evangelist, would have been the ones accustomed to describing their master as "the disciple whom Jesus loved," substituting this reverential title for John's "I" in the early, oral stages of gospel composition.[80]

Schnackenburg on Jn's Purpose and Style

An examination of Johannine speech patterns is shown to disclose, on the whole, Semitic rather than Greek rhetoric. (Schlatter's 1902 study assembling linguistic parallels to Jn in the Tannaitic-era Mekhilta on Exodus and Sifre on Deuteronomy is cited favorably, before a linguistic analysis of Johannine phrases having a Semitic coloration is provided.) This includes the method of concentric or, more properly, spiral exposition of a subject. Schnackenburg shows the extent of Jn's familiarity with Pharisaic and rabbinic Judaism as well as with language patterns that surface in the Qumrân texts. The author of Jn is said to be totally ignorant of Greco-Roman philosophy except for some terms that were in the public domain, like *logos* and "re-birth."

The evangelist's main interest is in belief in Jesus as Messiah in a way that transcends all previous expectations (his precosmic existence as Word not least); likewise, salvation by the exalted Christ as a present reality, expressed in a formula like "my flesh for the life of the world" (6:5); and intimate union with God through belief in Christ. He was above all a theologian who put the faith of his community in Jesus on the lips of Jesus.

As in any commentary, the author of this one seems to grow in sophistication and insight as he moves forward into the text. The technique of comment on verses and pericopes forbids a development of the evangelist's themes except for those places where the writer stops to make one. One finds in the first volume the familiar tendency to track down parallels to every word or phrase in the Bible, the Apocrypha, or Qumrân, creating the impression that the author thinks the evangelist *could* have been influenced by these scraps. Reflections on what a total pericope might have signified to its framer is thus drowned in minute etymological detail. Format and style change in volume 2, which appeared in German after a five-year interval. The bibliographical entries are much more current and on the target of the text. Those in volume 1 give evidence of long-term hoarding without much culling as publication came on. The commentary also begins to consist of lengthy reflections on the pericopes under consideration, far better developed and less fragmented than before. Thus, one could encounter in the early volume a footnote of this sort, imposing Christian ideas of Jesus as the Messiah on the unsuspecting eighth and seventh centuries BC: "The enquiring Pharisees [of 1:24–26] must have known that the Holy Spirit was part of the Messianic blessings (cf. Ezek 36:25f.; 37:5f.; 39:29; Joel 3:14f.; Is 32:15; 44:3; 59:21) and hence that a ritual merely of water fulfilled no Messianic function." Although blameless before John the Baptizer's appearance, Schnackenburg holds, they were surely at fault, on biblical grounds, in face of the preaching of Jesus.

Brown in a review of Schnackenburg wrote: "Thus far in the twentieth century this may well be the best full-scale commentary on a book of the New Testament written by a European Roman Catholic." One can concur in saying at least that much of Schnackenburg's achievement, perhaps more.

After Brown published his commentary on Jn (1966; 1970), he produced a steady stream of books, articles, and public lectures but also three works of exegetical commentary: *The Birth of the Messiah* (1977; rev. ed. 1993); *The Epistles of John* (1982); and *The Death of the Messiah* (2 vols., 1994). When death took him suddenly at seventy in 1998, he had planned a revision of *The Gospel According to John* and got as far as composing an introductory portion of some 280 pages. His publisher and the superior of his Society of St. Sulpice, diocesan priests engaged in seminary education, asked Francis J. Moloney to edit that work along with some supplementary notes. The result was *An Introduction to the Gospel of John* (New York: Doubleday, 2003). Moloney divides Brown's work into nine chapters with updated bibliographies for each, which he appears to have updated further. Moloney edits a clear, running prose that reports on the unity and composition of the FG, its relation to the Synoptics, its historicity, the influences upon it, its language and style, and crucial questions of Johannine theology. In nine "riders" (Moloney's term), Brown indicates a new, nuanced position on how Jesus might well have been in religious argument with fellow Jews in his lifetime—the Pharisee, pre-rabbinic period and how *hoi Ioudaioi* used in a hostile sense might have been the term of the Johannine church to designate not Jewish leaders but the emerging rabbinic Judaism with which it was in contest. One position that Brown did not adopt over the thirty-year interval was a narrative solution to questions that historical method could not answer, despite his modified commitment to it. The other was a coming to terms with metaphor and other symbolic language in Jn, especially in speech placed on Jesus' lips.

2
The Question of Sources

Rudolf Bultmann's 1941 commentary *The Gospel of John* provided a theory of the three major sources and an amorphous fourth on which the evangelist drew before the whole Gospel was edited and drastically rearranged by an "Ecclesiastical Redactor." **Eugen Ruckstuhl** seemed to refute its major contentions effectively a decade later.[1] He maintained that there were no written sources, since Johannine characteristics could be shown to prevail throughout the Fourth Gospel. The question lay dormant until 1958, when **Wilhelm Wilkens,** another Swiss, proposed a basic signs gospel, the work of the beloved disciple, who also later redacted it and added discourse material.[2] In a final editing the existing text was rearranged and further added to, with a Passover framework imposed on the whole that had not been present initially (see 2:13; 6:4; 11:55, which are followed by narratives that do not seem to fit these introductions). Wilkens gave more attention than Bultmann to method by stressing the contextual evidence pointing to successive editings of an initial source.

Reconstructing the Signs Source: Fortna

Meantime, Bultmann's one contention that survived with least challenge was that John had employed a "signs source" (SQ as he called it, for *Semeia-Quelle*). *Semeia* and sometimes *erga* ("works") were the terms in the FG for the miraculous deeds put forward in proof of Jesus' messiahship. Bultmann did not delineate them in any one place, referring to them in extended footnotes only as they occurred. D. M. Smith[3] submitted Bultmann's theory to a clear exposition and then critiqued it, but it remained for **R. T. Fortna** to do what Bultmann had failed to do. He provided a Greek text of the hypothetical signs source, going further than the master by finding it to be not merely a collection of miracle stories but a true gospel.[4] It had no teaching of Jesus, he concluded, but it did culminate in a passion and resurrection narrative.

Eduard Schwartz of Tübingen early in the twentieth century appears to have been the first to apply the Greek term *aporia* (lit. "block," "obstruction") to the Johannine material. It describes "the many inconsistencies, disjunctures and hard connections, even contradictions—which the text shows, notably in the narrative portions."[5] Seeing in these editorial seams evidence of insertion of material into a source, Fortna went on the hypothesis that the present Gospel was the (probably multiple) redaction of a basic text. Bultmann had provided him with a lead by identifying a tension between the actual accounts of Jesus' miraculous deeds (2:1–12; 4:46–54; 5:19; 6:1–13; 9:1–7; 11:1–44; 21:1–6) and the summaries and editorial comments that accompanied them. But Fortna observed that Bultmann brought preconceived theological and stylistic judgments into the discussion. Fortna thought this improper and confined himself to internal criteria. The chief criterion he employed was the existence of aporias in the miracle stories (reckoning the walking on water, 6:15–25, as one of them, as Bultmann had not). These he thought could best be explained as indicators of Johannine additions to a pre-Johannine source. Also, using the stylistic criteria of Ruckstuhl and Schweizer, he came to an opposite conclusion from theirs, namely, that the signs source was marked by peculiarities of language and style. This hypothetical source is more akin to Synoptic style than Johannine. Since it contains both miracle stories and a passion narrative, Fortna concluded that he had identified "a pre-Johannine stratum which had already a distinctive *literary* character imposed upon it."[6] Its author and audience seem to have been bilingual (Greek and Aramaic).[7] It was a missionary tract with a single end, to show (presumably to the potential Jewish convert) that Jesus is the Messiah.[8]

Employing certain punctuation marks, Fortna concludes his study by printing out in Greek what was in the source. Parentheses indicate passages that are not certainly to be assigned to it, square brackets enclose conjectural or uncertain readings, and double brackets are placed around passages whose place in the source is uncertain. The siglum I...I stands for places where Jn has made insertions into the source. The result is roughly the following (lacking the above indications and not listing parts of verses rather than whole verses where they occur):

Introduction

Exordium **1**:6, 7
The Baptist's testimony **1**:19–21, 23, 26, 27, 33, 32, 34
The conversion of the first disciples **3**:23–24; 1:35–50

The Signs of Jesus

1. *Water changed into wine* **2**:1–3, 5–11
2. *A nobleman's son healed* **2**:12a; 4:46b–47, 49–54
3. *A miraculous draught of fish* **21**:2–8b, 10–12, 14
4. *The multitude fed* **6**:1–3, 5, 7–14. *Interlude: walking on water* 15b–22, 25
5. *A dead man raised; a Samaritan woman* **11**:1–4, 7, 11, 15; 4:4–7, 9, 16–19, 25–26, 28–30, 40, 41; **11**:17–20, 28, 32–34, 38–39, 41–45
6. *A man blind from birth healed* **9**:1–3a, 6–8
7. *A thirty-eight-year illness healed* **5**:2–3, 5–9, 14

The Death and Resurrection of Jesus

The cleansing of the Temple and death plot **2**:14–16, 18–19; 11:47a, 53
The anointing of Bethany **12**:1–5, 7–8

The triumphal entry **12**:12–15

The Last Supper Fragments of the source's account in
12:27; **13**:(1b), 2a, 4–5, 12–14, 18b, 21b, 26–27, 37–38;
14:31b; **16**:32b

The arrest (**18**:1–5, 10–12); *Jesus in the high priest's house*
(**18**:13, 24, 15–16a, 19–23, 16b–18, 25b–28); *The trial
before Pilate* (**18**:28, 33, 37, 38c; **19**:15, **18**:39–40; **19**:6,
12–14a, 1–2, 16); *The crucifixion and burial* (**19**:16–19,
20b, 23–24, 28–29, 30b, 25, 31–34a, 36–38; **3**:1;
19:39–42)

The resurrection (**20**:1–3, 5, 7–11, 12, 14, 16–20)

Peroration **20**:30–31

If that seems to the casual reader little more than Bultmann's scissors-and-paste rearrangement of the Gospel, the
impression will be dispelled by a laborious examination of the
Greek. That discloses a remarkable consistency of vocabulary
and style in the putative source and yields a sequential narrative
that is not to be found in the canonical Fourth Gospel, interrupted
as it seems to be by many editorial insertions. The key to Fortna's
reconstruction is consistency. He eliminates any interruptions and
sudden turns, non sequiturs, doublets, and passages with dense or
overloaded wording.

Fortna's Revisions: The "Predecessor" of the Fourth Gospel

In a book produced almost two decades later, the Vassar College scholar revises his theory in light of the criticisms leveled at it
and his own testing of it by the use of slightly altered criteria.[9] This
longer and more explicit treatment deserts the Greek in favor of
transliteration. It divides the narrative source (SG for "signs
gospel") into twenty sections and employs a twofold typographical
aid: first, the hypothetical pre-Johannine source printed in boldface,
and then, in a reversal, the presumed redaction shown in boldface,

leaving the SG in ordinary type. The latter remains largely as it was in the earlier book. Taking the first chapter as an example, we find Fortna eliminating in his second book phrases and whole verses, leaving a source that opens with the "man…whose name was John" giving testimony to Jesus. He has no other role. He is God's agent through whom faith in Jesus is to arise. Jesus is not introduced by name in the SG. He is simply hailed by John as "the Lamb of God," and is identified as the Christ, Elijah, and the prophet by indirection. The climactic christological affirmation is that he is the Son of God.[10] Two disciples of John, Andrew and another unnamed, follow Jesus. Andrew leads Simon to Jesus and Jesus gives him a new name, Cephas. Andrew or Peter, not Jesus, is the "he" who finds the townsman of the two, Philip, in v. 43b. Philip finds Nathanael and calls Jesus the one of whom Moses wrote in the Law. (Fortna is unsure whether "and also the prophets" was in the source.) Nathanael hails Jesus as Rabbi, Son of God, and King of Israel.

What must be removed from ch. 1 of the Gospel as we have it, after its redaction by the fourth evangelist, in order to arrive at the signs gospel? The following elements: any repetitious or overexplicit details; "the Jews"; Jesus as one unknown, even by John; geographic and time-sequence specificity; theological elaborations, for example, Jesus as the one who "takes away the sin of the world" and the divinely revealed explanation to John of who he is on whom the dove-Spirit descends; Hebrew words translated into Greek; Nathanael's guilelessness, which is unlike Jacob-Israel's; Jesus' mysterious knowledge, both questioned and explained; and the obviously Johannine "Amen, amen" and "Son of Man," coupled with a second-person-plural, traditional saying addressed to Nathanael.

A careful breakdown by verses in each of the twenty segments follows both the "pre-Johannine source" (SG) and the "Johannine redaction" (4G). Concluding the segment is a more technical "Analysis" that justifies what has been declared redactional. Here, along with some tight argumentation based on grammar, style, and content, phrases proliferate such as "appears to be

Johannine" or "little doubt that it stems in some form from the Passion Source." Fortna had given himself at the outset a seven, on a scale of ten, for confidence in his own choices. He also modestly states that he should be happy if more than half of what he proposes is convincing to others.

His major conclusions are as follows: that a pre-Johannine document was employed by the fourth evangelist that presented seven or eight miracle stories as signs of Jesus' messiahship to make clear who Jesus is and for no other purpose; that there was pre-Johannine passion material that accounted for why Jesus the Messiah had to die by claiming that "these things happened to fulfill scripture"; that the fact that Jesus worked the signs of the Messiah means that the new age has appeared, there being no mention of future expectation in SG; and that, although Jesus does go from Galilee to Judea in SG, there is no interest in region (as distinct from place-names) as such, hence all negative reference to *Ioudaioi* ("Judeans" for Fortna) is added by the evangelist because of the harassment Christian Jews were experiencing from Jews more generally in his time and place.

Another Attempt to Recover the Gospel of Signs

Urban C. von Wahlde's attempt to isolate the first version of Jn appeared a year after Fortna's.[11] It bears the regretful note that, as *The Fourth Gospel and Its Predecessor* appeared after von Wahlde's book was in press, he could not discuss it in detail. But he does observe that Fortna sought only to analyze the redactional additions within the signs material, leaving the choices of *The Gospel of Signs* largely intact. Von Wahlde, of Chicago's Loyola University, sets about identifying signs material by applying these criteria: vocabulary or linguistic differences; thought-pattern or ideological differences (thirteen in number); four theological features; five minor characteristics useful in identifying signs material. Applying these to chs. 1–20 of the FG (and having decided that the miracle of 21:1–11 did not stem from the same tradition as the signs material), he arrives at thirty-seven pericopes found in chs. 1–7, 9–12, and 18–20.[12] The longest is of twenty-six verses (ch. 11); eight are of two or three verses only.

Von Wahlde's method does not begin with an examination of the miracle and passion narratives but goes from the aporias disclosing literary seams to the variation in vocabulary ("language") employed for the same realities. He then proceeds to elements of thought within the Gospel such as hostility to Jesus ("ideology"), which occur in ways contradictory or inconsistent with each other. Differences in religious thought ("theology") as between a first and second edition provide his third workable criterion. Taking his cue from Wellhausen, Spitta, and more modernly M. C. White,[13] von Wahlde in probing the FG's terms for religious authorities discovers that "Pharisees," "chief priests," and "rulers" occur consistently within one set of pericopes and "Jews" as a hostile term in another. The latter can also mean simply people who are Jews or Jews of the southern province, Judea, but in thirty-seven of its seventy-one occurrences in the Gospel it means those Jews set against Jesus.

Concentrating on the passages that feature this usage as contrasted with the other terms for Jewish authorities ("Pharisees," "chief priests," and "rulers," used singly or coupled), von Wahlde then applies his other criteria to the Jews-as-hostile pericopes. In the latter the word *erga* is always used for miracles, but in the three neutral descriptions of authorities, *sēmeia*. "Sign" always has the positive meaning of miracle except in 2:18 and 6:30 (where Jesus is challenged to perform a sign defensively as proof, both times in conjunction with "Jews," 2:18 and 6:41). "Works" is a word for miracles in passages that employ "Jews"; but it also bears the dualistic meaning from apocalyptic writing of doing the will of God or the devil. Jesus describes his ministry as a whole as "work" (4:34; 17:4). Examples of the coupling of "signs" and neutral terms like "ruler of the Jews," "Pharisees," and "chief priests" occur in 3:1–2; 7:31–32; 9:16. Such passages become, for von Wahlde, the building blocks of the first edition of the FG. Contrariwise, in 5:15 and 10:24–38 "Jews" is used in conjunction with the verb "work" and the noun "works." This twofold correlation of signs/authorities and works/Jews is both consistent and exclusive throughout the Gospel. Separate authorship of two strands of writing is concluded to be the key, not "works" on the lips of Jesus only as some had previously thought.[14] The one exception to the works/Jews pattern is 6:26, even though "Jews" does not occur in the passage until vv. 41 and 52. "Jews" refers to the territory of Judea in 3:22 and means Judeans in 3:25 (its sole occurrence in the singular); 11:19, 31, 33, 36, 45, 54; 12:9, 11; 19:20. In these places there is mention of Judea or Jerusalem and no note of hostility attaches to it. More importantly, the occurrences in chs. 11, 12, and 19 are in conjunction with the terms "Pharisees," "chief priests," and "rulers."

Adding Ideology and Theology to Vocabulary as Criteria for the Signs Gospel

Von Wahlde terms this distinct, twofold usage his primary linguistic criterion. A secondary one that "checks out" when applied to passages determined by it or identified by ideological and theological criteria as belonging to the signs source is that words that refer to Jewish religious concepts are first given in Hebrew, then in Greek (1:38, 41, 42; 2:23; 20:16), while place-names are generally given first in Greek, then in Hebrew (Aramaic): 5:2; 19:13, 17. An exception is 6: 1, which is a juxtaposition rather than a translation. Of the above, only 2:23, 5:2, and 6:1 occur in passages determined by the first or linguistic criterion.

The Earliest Version goes on to uncover ten differences in thought or perspective between the signs material and the remainder of the Gospel. These include stereotyped formulas of immediate or easy belief ("and his disciples/many/even of the rulers/the Judeans, believed in him"), emphasis on the number and greatness of the signs, emphasis on the variety of groups that come to believe in Jesus, and the hostility of the Pharisees as something that increases slowly and is marked by unsuccessful action (7:32) and uncertainty (12:19), then a final, decisive move (18:3). There is a division of opinion regarding Jesus in the signs material. In it, too, narrative predominates, punctuated by brief exchanges, but there are no extended discourses. Theologically, belief is based on the performance of signs in this material and it is presented as following easily upon the miracle, even though not all capitulate in faith (see the holding back of some "authorities," the probable "they" of 12:37), while other Sanhedrin members believe (v. 42a). This first or "Jewish-authorities" edition presents belief in Jesus within the categories of a traditional Christology such as "from God" (3:2; 9:33), "a prophet" (4:19), "the prophet" (6:14), "Messiah" (1:41; 4:25). In the early edition, too, the supernatural knowledge of Jesus functions to bring about belief, as in the cases of Nathanael (1:47–49) and the Samaritan woman (4:16–19, 39). Jesus possesses such knowledge in the second edition but it functions differently: to show his sovereign superiority to all things human (thus, 2:24–25; 6:15, 64; 18:4–9).

If all the usages in the above paragraph characterize the earliest version of the FG, which employs the terms "Pharisees," "chief priests," and "rulers" for the Jewish authorities, the second edition marked by "Jews" in a hostile sense has these features: ethnic Jews fear "the Jews" (7:13; 9:22; 20:19); the "works" that Jesus performs, which he himself has to draw attention to, serve as testimony but have little (5:36) or no (10:32) effect; Jesus' opponents, "the Jews," are bitterly hostile to him from the start—there is no sense of building climax (2:18–22; 5:10–20)—even seeking to stone (8:59; 10:31) or to kill him (5:18; 7:1; 11:8); "the Jews" are never divided over Jesus (see 9:18–23) nor are the people described as being divided over him; dialogue and discourse material (2:18–22, 5:10–47; 6:30–59; 7:14–19, 33–36; 8:13–29, 48–59; 10:22–39) largely overtakes narrative; Jesus' "works" become but one of four witnesses to him; a high Christology that identifies Jesus with God (5:18; 8:58; 10:33) replaces the traditional messianic titles.

Von Wahlde concludes that, despite the limitations of his enterprise, there is much that can be known of the structure and theology of the signs material. Central to it are the number and power of Jesus' signs, which increase in magnitude (going from the earliest healings to that of the man *born* blind and the raising of Lazarus). The people's belief and the hostility of the authorities grow commensurately, Although christologically God is spoken of as being with Jesus, who is both a prophet and Messiah, Jesus performs all the signs by his own authority. The clearest background for the Johannine signs is that of the description in Exodus and Numbers of the signs given to Moses, as the studies of Teeple (1957), Glasson (1963), and Meeks (1967) had already shown. But Moses typology is not paramount in the signs source. Rather, Jesus is mainly depicted there as the expected one of Israel, its Messiah (1:41; 4:25, 29), king (1:49), and Son of God (1:49). As Messiah, "no one will know where he comes from" (7:27), yet it cannot be conceived that Jesus has performed fewer signs than the Messiah will at his coming (v. 31). Christ or prophet, the signs amply sustain his title to being both. The Gospel's Christology, judging from what remains to us, focuses almost exclusively on the importance of the miraculous.

From Neutrality to Hostility:
A New Christology in the Second Edition of the SG

There is no polemic against John in the signs source. He is shown simply as one who testified to Jesus, being neither the Christ, Elijah, nor the prophet. Unlike Jesus, he "did no sign" (10:41). The signs gospel is Jewish and traditional, written for Jews against a backdrop of their standard view of Moses. It relates details of Jesus' life that we know from no other source, including the affinity of his career with the Baptist movement. It is a document that shows familiarity with numerous locales in Palestine, religious customs, and feasts (Sukkoth, 7:2, and Ḥanukkah, 10:22, besides Pesaḥ). We cannot accurately construct from it the number of Jesus' trips to Judea but it catalogues his extensive activity there, chiefly in Jerusalem. The signs gospel was proclamational rather than apologetic. It originated in perhaps 70–80 CE in "association with the southern part of Palestine."[15] The same community from which it came probably produced the second edition. Of its author nothing can be known from within the reconstructed text.

The second stage of the community's history lets us know about a bitter struggle over exclusion of the Jesus-believing Jews from the synagogue. Von Wahlde assigns 9:18–23, which contains *aposynágōgos,* a word of uncertain precision (v. 22), to the middle of the three editions[16] and supposes that it has been added to 12:42 by redaction.[17] This second edition has assigned a symbolism to Jesus' signs different from the reason for their presence in the signs gospel (see 6:26–58, the synagogue instruction on bread at Capernaum; 9:35–41, a spiritual meaning given to blindness and sight; 11:25b–26, a similar interpretation of Lazarus's resuscitation and new life). The redacted version of the first edition speaks of belief as if it has a deeper foundation than simply seeing signs. There are other "witnesses" (a term used in this second edition), but one cannot respond to any of them with belief unless one possesses the Spirit. The Nicodemus episode (3:3–21 added in the second edition to 2:23; 3:1–2 of the signs gospel) makes this clearest of all. Jesus is here calling for a new form of existence. The same is true of the addition of 4:10–15, 20–24, 31–38, 40–42 in the story of the Samaritan woman. Of ch. 7, only 25–27, 31–32, 40–52 are from the signs gospel; the remainder is probably from the second edition but may come from the third, to which von Wahlde assigns the discussion of Jesus' "whence" and "whither": earthly origin/heavenly origin; the diaspora/his return to the Father.

In the first edition the disciples are presented as responding properly to each of the four witnesses of Jesus: to John (1:35–49); to the sign at Cana (2:1–11); to the scriptures (2:13–17, 22); to the word of Jesus (2:18–22). They then largely disappear from the narrative until the Last Supper. The theology of the second edition, which sees the possession of the Spirit as the basis for all believing response to Jesus, conceives the giving of the Spirit, nonetheless, as taking place only after Jesus is glorified (7:37–39; 20:22). The Christology of the second edition probably reaches its peak in 10:22–39. It is there that in response to the query whether he is the Messiah he speaks of God as "my Father" and claims to be "God's Son," saying, "I and the Father are one" and "the Father is in me and I in him." There, too, he is challenged with "making himself equal to God."

The recovered "earliest version" of the book's title can be read through in sequence in chapter 3, going from one pericope to the next. Of the thirty-seven in all, eight are in the passion narrative. The one risen-life pericope is the appearance to Mary Magdalene. Setting the various terms for Jewish authorities in boldface ("Jews" only in the meaning "Judeans") identifies the primary criterion of selection. Unlike some other source sleuths, von Wahlde unhesitatingly assigns connective phrases of time and place to his source. He does not claim that the portions of the signs gospel that have survived to the canonical John are its complete form. Neither does he presume to say what editing it may have undergone, only the basic changes it did not undergo as it proceeded to a second and a third edition (the Jn that we have). The attentive reader will naturally be on guard to find exceptions that fall outside his generalizations and will examine with care his reasons for assigning passion and risen-life narratives to the signs source.[18] He constantly refers to his differences from Bultmann, Brown, Fortna, Boismard-Lamouille, and others who track the FG's sources or redactional stages so that judgments can be made on their respective arguments. If he is right, even in fair measure, then much has been resolved about puzzling sequences, abrupt changes in style and content, and above all the distressing hostility to "the Jews" in the FG. For, like Brown and Fortna, von Wahlde ascribes its bitter tone to an editing that came after the grave harassment and even ejection of the Jesus-believing Jews from ordinary Jewish life, somewhere in Palestine he would say.

The Contributions of Smith, Martyn, and Lindars

D. Moody Smith is, in a sense, the dean of U.S. Johannine specialists, as much through the dissertations he has directed and the teaching careers he has launched as through his articles and scholarly lectures. He published a collection of his writings produced between 1961 and 1981, for which he wrote an introductory essay, "Johannine Christianity."[19] After reviewing the results of various modes of analysis of the FG, such as the redaction-critical,[20] he identifies the greater part of the discourse or sayings material as forming the basis for what is truly Johannine. By this he means the work of the evangelist who preceded the final redactor. For Smith 1 Jn has the same "distinctively Johannine ring." It is but a short step from the Paraclete passages of 14:25–26 and 16:12–15 "to the conjecture that the words of Jesus in the Fourth Gospel, so obviously spoken from the standpoint of a Spirit-inspired post-resurrection community (cf. John 7:39; 20:22), are to be regarded as the fulfillment of the promise of the Paraclete rather than the words of the historical Jesus."[21]

Smith notes his agreement in principle with the identification of an independent Johannine narrative tradition, if not Fortna's gospel of signs, and points to mounting evidence for the existence of a Johannine discourse tradition as well.[22] He remains in an older mold of Jn scholarship with his statement that the miracle tradition may embody a *theios anēr*[23] Christology from a pre-gospel collection that may be called an aretalogy. The same can be said of his judgment that "it…does not seem possible to explain the entire history of the Johannine tradition against such a background [Judaism and the outlook of Christian Jews]."[24] Yet twenty years before, he had reported "a loose, but real, consensus" on the fundamentally Semitic and even Jewish character of the Johannine tradition and preaching.[25] Smith is at ease distinguishing between a cycle of miracle stories existing independently from a passion narrative, the former probably originating among those who had been disciples of the Baptist and directed to this sect to get them to change allegiance, the latter to convince Jews generally that Jesus was the Messiah, as a signs source alone would not have succeeded in doing.[26]

Raymond E. Brown refers to a "strong current movement rejecting a proposed pre-Johannine Signs-source gospel"[27] in reviewing a recent dissertation from the University of Basel.[28] The author, **W. J. Bittner,** examines the term *sēmeîon* at length, prompted by its nonuse in the Synoptic tradition. He attributes Jn's peculiar positive use of it, not to that Gospel's drawing on a prophet-like-Moses theme, but on the strongly Davidic Isaiah 11. This Isaian background of the usage of Jn, who employs signs positively to elicit faith in Jesus as Christ and Son of God, is Bittner's main thesis.

J. Louis Martyn wrote a very influential book in the period just after our starting date of 1965 but revised it in a second edition well into that decade.[29] In it he concluded that Jn 9 (and 5 and 7 like it) was a two-level drama constructed by the evangelist in which the man born blind was a Jew of Jerusalem who was also made to represent those Jewish members of the separated church in an unidentified Diaspora city. Its messianic faith in Jesus, as a result of his miracles, led to their ejection from the synagogue. Martyn understands this as a formal excommunication resulting from the "awesome [twelfth] Benediction" of the *Shemone Esre* (Eighteen) which declared *minim*—a word he translates "heretics"—to be accursed. In his reconstruction, the academy at Yavneh under Gamaliel II had inserted that curse sometime around 85 and it was being used to catch believers in Jesus as Messiah. Since no previous Jewish writing had said that the Messiah would be a wonder-worker, Jesus could have been no more than a magician, a deceiver, or so the emerging rabbinate thought. He was accused of leading people astray (Jn 7:12, 47), a charge that Martyn takes to mean entice *(yasāth)* them to believe in more than one God. A passage from the Mishnah of ca. 180 *(Sanhedrin* 7, 10–11) lumps together "enticing to idolatry" with the promise of wonders, *leading astray* (see Deut 13:2–3, 6), and *practicing sorcery* or magic, as deeds deserving death. The accusation on such charges was being made against believers in Jesus as the result of a rabbinic decree that went out to Diaspora synagogues as early as the writing of Jn. A *baraita* (= "outside" the Mishnah) of the period 200–400, describing the hanging and stoning of Yeshu on the eve of the Passover on the above three charges, is also presented as evidence *(Sanhedrin* 43a). The Johannine community, knowing that the performance of signs was no part of messianic expectation, had apparently been casting Jesus in the mold of the prophet like Moses (Deut 18:15) who gave bread from the heavens. It did not save them, however, from harassment unto death for claiming they knew the Messiah to be a crucified wonder-worker, for the terms were wrong.

In a paper presented in 1975, Martyn continued to be convinced that the curse on a Jew who had a soft policy on God's oneness (a *min*) corresponded to that person's becoming or being declared *aposynágōgos* (Jn 9:22; 12:42; 16:2).[30] This "highly probable correspondence" becomes within the same paragraph a *"Festpunkt"* (fixed or basing point). Following from it, the argument is presented that underlying Jn 1:35–40 is a homily directed to Jews of the kind meant by Paul when he spoke of a "gospel of the circumcision" (Gal 2:7). Someone, probably the evangelist John, had edited it awkwardly to make Jesus take the initiative in calling Philip (v. 43) as he does with the apostles in the other Synoptics. The early homilist, however, had portrayed men who *came* (vv. 39, 46, 47) to Jesus and *found* (vv. 41, 45) him to be the Messiah. In the same way, the preacher hoped that many hearers would come and find Jesus.

The early period represented by this pericope before its editing was marked by much success. Jews were preaching Jesus to Jews in a synagogue framework and many came to believe in him (see 2:11; 4:53; 6:14). The group of believers "experienced no social dislocation and felt relatively little alienation from their heritage."[31] The middle period followed upon excommunication from the synagogue and some martyrdoms, making the group into a separate community. The Logos hymn is probably to be assigned to this period. As Martyn paraphrases the situation, "The Messiah came to his own world, / and his own people did *not* receive him."[32] The late period witnessed further homilies but also the climactic writing of the full Johannine Gospel in its first and second editions. In this matter Martyn concurs with his Union Theological Seminary colleague Brown in his five-stage analysis. The authorities had evidently laid down the dictum in the middle period, Jesus or Moses, and believers in Jesus had opted for him as their (late-period, Greek-designated) "Christ." The "Jewish Christians" have thus come into existence; "Christian Jews" remain undeclared, in the synagogues. The "other sheep not of this fold" are the latter group, who are "of the world" (see 8:31ff., 12:42).

Barnabas Lindars authored a commentary on Jn in the New Century Bible,[33] at the conclusion of which he delivered four lectures, published earlier, containing some of the ideas expressed in it.[34] These ideas on Johannine traditions he continued to hold in his Leuven lecture at the same conference as Martyn's above.[35] In agreement with Brown (on pp. XXXIV–LI), as Lindars puts it, he assumes that "the gospel is based on the evangelist's own sermons, which he has united to form the complete book."[36] Despite the temporal aporias, the thematic breaks, and the recurring pattern of signs (each of them constituting an epiphany of the divine man)—all of which Lindars acknowledges—there is a prima facie case for supposing that Jn "began life as separate homilies, which the evangelist subsequently used as the basis for a continuous Gospel. The discourse, then, is not a report of an actual debate....It is rather a sermon addressed to the Christians in order to deepen and strengthen their faith in a situation where Jewish objections to Christianity [*sic*] are a matter of vital concern."[37]

Oscar Cullmann's *The Johannine Circle* suggests the following process of composition: The author, a strong personality, called on common traditions and others special to him, not excluding personal reminiscences, producing the main lines of the work as we have it now. A circle of redactors or a single one revised or completed the whole work after his death, most likely in Syria or Transjordania.[38] We shall be returning to this book below (p. 49) to see what Cullmann thinks about Samaritans in the Jn community.

A "Priority" That Does Not Mean First to Be Composed

Before leaving the question of sources of the FG, a report must be filed on that work of two decades ago that denied most vehemently that John, son of Zebedee (who wrote Jn), drew on any sources. It is **Bishop John A. T. Robinson**'s *The Priority of John,* in effect a detailed discussion of the entire Gospel. The book does not hold as its main thesis what the title might suggest, namely, that Jn was composed in toto before the other three.[39] Robinson's considerably more nuanced position is that his title "does not necessarily mean the temporal priority of John" but the case for a "procedural" priority — a complete openness to such temporal priority, to be sure, "though I should be inclined to think that the writing that went into the Fourth Gospel may well have begun earlier *and* gone on later than in the case of the others."[40] That sentence is the tip-off to the amount of openness the bishop is willing to allow. He does not wish to deal with one formal interdependence among the four gospels, that is, the literary. That he rightly describes as a problem that no longer looms large in scholarly perspective. But the interrelatedness of the four gospels is something he thinks will not go away.

He opts for the position that Jn was "a primary source in whose light they too [the Synoptics] can be viewed."[41] This is put forward as a hypothesis, a means of exploring what happens if one reverses the prevailing assumption that Jn is not a primary source. As to source criticism of the Fourth Gospel, Robinson has a poor opinion of it. He seems happy to quote an opinion of Kysar on the contents of the signs source/gospel as proposed by Teeple, Fortna *(TGOS),* Nicol, Schnackenburg, and Jürgen Becker, that "source criticism is 'somewhat in shambles.'"[42] No matter that Kysar had limited his observation to method in source criticism. For Robinson the outcome is in no better condition than the method employed.

He engages in a book-length polemic against the idea that the FG "is so remote in time from the situation it describes that it could not credibly in any sense be a first Gospel."[43] The bishop sees no reason to depart in this, the last book of his life, from his earlier proposed chronology of the composition of Jn spelled out in *Redating the New Testament.*[44] There he had argued for the following rough stages:

30–50	Shaping of the gospel material in dialogue with Palestinian Judaism
50–55	Preaching in the Ephesus area and the first edition of the Gospel
60–65	The epistles, responding to the challenges of false teachers
65+	Second edition of the Gospel with prologue and epilogue[45]

Historical Happenings, Not Documents, as Jn's Source

It seems quite unproven to Robinson that John depended on sources. The FG for him gives no indication of standing in an external and secondhand relation to other elements of a tradition that its author took over, making use of it and working on it. At the heart of his argumentation is the question of historicity. He grants that this is independent of the matter of establishing sources, but it is "certainly not irrelevant to the question of whether John goes back to source rather than sources."[46] The interrelation of tradition and event, however complex it may be, is not so simple as to say that the question of that relation can only be raised after the literary task of separating redaction from tradition is complete.[47] "The presumption is surely justified that an underlying event has at some point controlled the reports rather than simply the reports each other."[48] Thus, the historicity of Nicodemus and of Martha and Mary of Bethany is much better accounted for by the fact that there were such persons to whom such things happened—divergent descriptions being a common event—than that (in the latter case) John and Luke were using each other or some underlying source. Robinson maintains in the same discussion that there are "basically three *independent* traditions of the trial and death of Jesus, the Markan, the Lukan and the Johannine, and that each goes back, directly or indirectly to source."[49] "Source" is what happened in history retained in different traditional tellings, as is the case with reports on events in life generally. History never quite puts us in touch with the facts, he makes clear, but with somebody's (or somebody else's) version of the facts (in a quotation from A. H. N. Green-Armytage of 1952). If this seems a cavalier dismissal of the immensely complex problem of gospel composition, Robinson challenges the reader to cope with his forest of arguments in favor of gospel events' having happened as described. The Johannine version is presented as being at least as trustworthy historically as any other, and without demonstrable dependence on a Synoptic account.

The Gospel according to John is a primary source. That is Robinson's first, last, and foremost contention. It is "at any rate *a* first written statement of the gospel, of primal rather than secondary significance."[50] He thinks "in fact that all the gospels were coming into being over a period more or less simultaneously, and at different stages their traditions and their redaction could well

show signs of mutual influence—as well as, of course, among the
Synoptists, of common written sources."[51] This is a way of
acknowledging the validity of the great body of gospel scholarship with which Robinson is familiar while holding fast to the priority of John. The latter means "begin[ning] with what John has
to tell us on its own merits and ask[ing] how the others fit, historically and theologically, into that, are illumined by it, and in turn
illumine it."[52] The best of all scholarly worlds is not repudiated by
such a claim, even as the claimant holds fast to his basic conviction: no sources behind John except what happened, as John successively interpreted these happenings.

In an evenhanded estimate of Robinson's performance—
something he did not always receive from his critics in life—D.
Moody Smith points out correctly that he is more at pains to make
the case for Jn's independence and historicity than its priority.[53] In
the matter of that second concern, many of his historical-critical
judgments are deemed "plausible or possible (e.g., [his] affirmation of John's two-year ministry and passion chronology against
the Synoptics). Few, if any, are fantastic." Yet Smith underscores
that Robinson is always the controversialist and advocate, never
the neutral arbiter of the data.

One needs to be clear before tackling this large and somewhat undisciplined book if one wants to follow the author in his
determination that everything in Jn can be shown to go back to
source (meaning Jesus) rather than to intermediate traditional
sources. Bishop Robinson had prepared a draft of eight chapters for the Bampton Lectures series, which C. F. D. Moule then
delivered as Robinson was dying. A sterner hand by the editor,
J. F. Coakley, would have made it a better book, but he may
have thought he had no such mandate with regard to the final
testament of this champion of the British tradition in biblical
scholarship.

"Circle" or "School"? Cullmann and Culpepper

The real importance of Cullmann's *The Johannine Circle* cited above probably lies in its contention that ch. 4 tells us much about the outreach of Hellenistic missionaries to Samaria. The exchange by Jacob's well was "an event in the life of Jesus and at the same time [an indication of] its extension in the work performed by the exalted Christ in his church."[54] Luke in Acts 8 reports on a mission to the town of Samaria led by the Greek-speaking Jew Philip (6:5) which, despite the Simon incident, was marked by considerable success (see 8:8, 25). Cullmann thinks that the evangelization of Samaria had to transcend the thorny question of the correct site for worship, as its sanctuary on Mount Gerizim might still have been in use. By putting the prophecy of a future mission to Samaria on Jesus' lips in a conversation with a Samaritan woman, Jn may be legitimizing it in circles where it is disputed ("Do not go into the cities of Samaria," Mt 10:5). Jesus planted the seed. ("They [the people of Sychar] left the town and came to him," 4:30.) The true harvest would be gathered only after his death. In Cullmann's reconstruction, vv. 37b–38 say:

> "One sows, another reaps."[55]
> I sent you to reap
> what you had not worked for.
> Others [than Jesus, viz., the Hellenists of Ac 6–8] have
>   done the labor,
> and you [Peter and John, for the Jerusalem church, Ac 8:14]
>   have come into their gain

Cullmann says he was the first to call attention to the link between the Hellenists of Acts — the Stephen party — and Jn.[56] His theory is that Jn is crediting Greek-speaking ethnic Jews of a heterodox bent (his term) as the true missionaries of Samaria, not the Jerusalem apostles, which is the tendency of Acts.

Doctoral dissertations can enshrine important research, usually on a topic that has not previously been isolated or examined with such care. **R. Alan Culpepper,** working under Moody Smith at Duke University, decided that the scholarly world had been using the term "the school of John" without precision ever since Renan first coined it more than a century ago, and he wondered if the usage was valid. He examined nine circles of study from the ancient world to which the term *school* has been applied or, by the criteria that emerged, can be.[57] Five represent pagan learning and four Jewish: the Pythagorean school, the Academy (Plato), the Lyceum (Aristotle), the Garden (Epicurus), the Stoa (Zeno), the school at Qumrân (the righteous teacher), the house of Hillel, Philo's school (a deduction), and the school of Jesus. Most of the schools examined shared nine characteristics.[58] When the word was applied to the Gospel and the epistles of John, but without taking Revelation into account or adopting a firm stand on authorship, Culpepper concluded it was right to speak of a Johannine "school" on the model of the others.

Its characteristics were the following.[59] (1) It was a "fellowship" of "disciples" ("brothers," "friends"), first of Jesus, then students taught about Jesus by the "beloved disciple." (2) This BD led and guided the Johannine community, going back to its beginnings. (3) The founder's traditions and teachings were reckoned the true interpretations of the words and deeds of Jesus and the meaning of the scriptures; as collected by the evangelist, they could be called a "writing." (4) Members of the community were disciples or students of the founder, the BD (see "we," 21:24). (5) Teaching, learning, studying (the scriptures), and writing were common activities in the community, which (6) observed a communal meal, and had (7) rules or practices regulating admission and retention of membership. (8) The community kept some distance from society ("the world") in a progressive withdrawal (1 Jn 2:19; and see Jn 15:18; 16:2; 17:9). (9) It also developed organizational means of ensuring its perpetuity, from the death of the BD onward. Culpepper's most arguable conclusion is that the BD, who was not the evangelist, as he assumes 19:34b–35 establishes, has by analogy the same relation to Jesus that Jesus had to the Father (3:35; 15:9). More than this, he fulfilled the role in the community that the Gospel's Paraclete sayings predict the Paraclete would. "Just as Jesus had been the first Paraclete for the original group of disciples, so the BD had been the first Paraclete for the Johannine community....After the BD died, it was necessary to affirm that the BD was not...the only Paraclete, but that the Paraclete was Spirit (14:26) and that he would remain always (14:17)."[60] The evangelist thus combined, apparently for the first time, the concepts of Paraclete and Spirit, reassuring the community that although their Paraclete, the BD, had died, the work of the Paraclete would continue.

The Who, Where, and Why of the Gospel and the Letters

The last word in this chapter should go to **Martin Hengel,** if only because his *The Johannine Question* gives the impression that it is the last word. What is the Johannine question?[61] It is: Who wrote the Gospel and the letters, where, and why? The answer? John the elder, who was the head of a school in Asia Minor between 60/70 and 100/110. He had gone there from Palestine to flee the Jewish War, perhaps came from a family of priestly aristocrats, was in contact with Jesus as his disciple as a young man, and lived to a great age. He could not have been John the son of Zebedee, who was the second in the earliest community after Peter, but he did model himself after that "disciple whom Jesus loved" and later fused the image of that John with his own.[62] "How far the specific 'beloved disciple' passages go back wholly to him and how far they are partially shaped by the redactional work of the editor(s) is hard to decide."[63] There was, in any case, an idealization of the son of Zebedee by John the elder, whose pupils impressed on the enigmatic figure of the BD *their* teacher.

The school at Ephesus founded by this impressive "disciple of the Lord" (so Papias) could have produced the Apocalypse after the Neronian persecution and reworked it early in the reign of Trajan. The Gospel grew slowly. Because it was directed against the Petrine-Synoptic tradition, it was published toward the end of the elder's life, with ch. 17 added later and the prologue last. We cannot tell its stages or the author's literary sources, but the whole is a literary unit (Ruckstuhl and Schweizer are right against Bultmann, Richter, and Fortna). The alterations and corrections were constant and his pupils left his inconsistencies in place, "perhaps...even...as a provocation!"[64] In part this was because the ongoing teaching was oral and the Gospel was but a testamentary by-product left late in life. Some of the elder's former pupils created a crisis by finding the Christology of the school untenable in light of the divine immutability and impassibility. Their secession elicited the three letters and such portions of the Gospel as the prologue, chs. 6 and 10, and passages in the farewell discourses.[65]

The scholarship reflected in Hengel's eighty-five pages of notes is a treasure trove, whatever one may think of the conclusions he comes to. Especially important is his marshaling of the second-century evidence on Johannine authorship and on the nonespousal of Jn by any Gnostic group except the Valentinian Christians. The problematical "synod of Jamnia" and the even more doubtful expulsion of Christians from the synagogue via the Eighteen Benedictions is well dealt with in a discussion of Jewish persecution of Christians, especially in Asia Minor.[66]

3
John as Religious Literature

It is possible to catch glimpses of the history of the Johannine community (or of late first-century life in a corner of the empire) through the window of John's Gospel, but the evangelist's writing is not primarily history, it is a story. It tells the story of a man and what happened to him, what he said and what he did, whom he related to and how he ended—and will never end. Because Jesus is believed in by many with religious faith as godhead in humanity, there has always been a certain hesitation to view the gospel stories as stories. They have been praised for their narrative power but more often viewed as repositories of revealed doctrine. Because the genre of history was so much to the fore in the years around 1800, asking whether or not a thing happened as described, the most serious New Testament study of the last two centuries has been historical. Only lately has it become literary in any sense other than the tracking of sources. Sometimes expositors of the Bible use the phrase "critical-historical" but that is a tautology. Until now the one has meant the other—at least in biblical study.

But an art critic is not a historian. Neither is a literary critic. Both exercise their critical faculties by describing how art objects speak to them, to people of refined taste, to people generally. The literary critic is shocked to learn that literary criticism means, to the Bible scholar, approaching "a text with, so to say, a dissecting knife in his hand, looking out particularly for breaks in continuity…for disturbing duplications…and for variations in the use of language in different parts of the text, all of them leading to, not appreciation of its merit, but a determination of sources."[1] It must be admitted, conversely, that literary critics have shied away from practicing their art on biblical narratives apart from attention to a few lively tales like the encounter between David and Goliath. Sacred and profane have long inhabited different worlds, even when the two are engaged in the same enterprise.

Petersen and Rhoads are two U.S. scholars who broke the silence with their studies of Mark as a narrative, employing the rhetorical analysis of Czech, Russian, British, and American students of the storyteller's art.[2] Rhoads collaborated with a colleague in literary studies. Meanwhile, Frank Kermode in England and Northrop Frye in Canada, neither one trained in the Bible, produced works of criticism on biblical material, Kermode on Mark's Gospel in particular.[3]

The Beginnings of a Genuine Literary Criticism of Jn: Culpepper

A few essays on Johannine irony and symbolism had preceded **David W. Wead**'s Basel dissertation on Jn's literary techniques[4] but it remained for **Alan Culpepper** to produce a thorough exploration of Jn as literary art.[5] The historically oriented New Testament scholars already had a term to describe it, "composition criticism," meaning an evangelist's work as author rather than editor. But they did not have in mind the highly developed art of narrative criticism, of the existence of which they were barely aware. Culpepper dove deeply into the literary critical studies of such well-regarded figures as Booth, Chatman, Genette, Scholes and Kellogg, Sternberg, and Uspensky. He asked, "What are they saying about narrative?" to learn what this writing might have to say about Jn. Like those who had analyzed Mk before him (and Kingsbury, Mt after him),[6] Culpepper methodically explored the following categories as they applied to Jn: narrator and point of view, narrative time, plot, characters, implicit commentary, and the implied reader.

Carefully examining Jn's twenty-one chapters under these aspects, Culpepper found its first hearers invited to enter a literary world created by the author from materials drawn from life and history, imagination and reflection. Jn "speaks retrospectively, telling a story that is a sublime blend of historical tradition and faith."[7] In this story the narrator (the voice Jn assumes in telling the story) shares the point of view of the actual author (who in taking on the role of author is called "the implied author"). He is as if omniscient and hence is not a character in the story; he breaks in on it throughout with helpful explanations and reminders; and he is entirely reliable in his judgments on persons and events. The hearer is thus inclined from the outset to adopt the narrator's view of Jesus and the response of others to him. The narrator does this by situating the story's place in history between "the beginning" (1:1) and "the last day" (6:40). He is also fully aware of the "whence" and "whither" of Jesus (6:46; 13:36; 16:5) as one who comes forth as Word-in-flesh from the bosom of the Father, and has gone back to the one who has sent him. The characters in the Gospel are sharply defined by "their response to Jesus, by the measure of their ability to believe, and by their progress toward or away from the perspective of the narrator."[8] Some reject him, others refuse to confess their faith openly, a few are caught between Jesus and his opponents and must choose whom to follow. The disciples, who react to his "glory" with belief, represent a variety of perceptions of Jesus that must be overcome. Only "the disciple whom Jesus loved" (Culpepper is silent on Jesus' mother in 2:5) is portrayed as responding with belief and love from the first we hear of him (13:23). He is the true witness to Jesus, the model of authentic faith. To hear this Gospel with its characters' various reactions to Jesus is not only to enter its narrative world but to be moved to consider one's own response. The narrator has an ideal and employs the BD to dramatize it. His message is: Overcome as he did whatever lack of understanding of Jesus you have and Jesus will be able to call you, too, disciple and friend; let my ironies get to you as they successively unmask the folly of disbelief and misperception.

The Beloved Disciple as Literary Image of the Narrator

Those to whom this Gospel was first directed must have felt the beliefs they held dear clarified and reaffirmed by it. A few were doubtless disconfirmed and angered by the narrator, identified by Culpepper as, in some sense, the beloved disciple. The Gospel must have sustained the former as they found themselves a part of the "we" who had beheld Jesus' glory. Little of that impact has been lost with the centuries, as the cumulative effect of the Gospel's rich and powerful narrative is felt by hearers in every age. Plot development is rather loose in this Gospel; the rapid progression from scene to scene is best described as episodic. But the FG has a unity and coherence that comes with the way it develops its few themes. The subtle elements of its narrative structure prove more powerful than the obvious ones. At the end, the evangelist's literary world sufficiently touches the real world of many readers that "they can accept his vision of the world as the true, the authentic *(alēthinos)* one."[9]

Erich Auerbach is quoted as saying on an early page in his *Mimesis,* "The world of the Scripture stories is not satisfied with claiming to be a historically true reality—it insists that it is the only real world." As long as any contemporary, post-Enlightenment readers insist on seeing in Jn a window on the ancient world, telling exactly what happened during Jesus' ministry, they can never see truth in it. Only when the FG is used as a mirror held up to readers' lives, as the narrator intended, can there be interaction with the glory of Jesus it discloses. This book has to be read or heard as literature because, like everything in the Bible, it is literature. It is art and history, it is fiction and truth, all reconciled in the evangelist's deft performance. If these are reconciled *in* the hearers' lives and *with* their lives, Jn can speak to them.

Culpepper says it is no part of his purpose to clarify Jn's composition history. In its present form it is a unity, a literary whole. Its deliberate construction of credibility through appeal to tradition, eyewitness testimony, inspiration (the Paraclete), the authority of an esteemed figure (the BD), and the multiplication of geographic and historical detail cumulatively confirms the claims the narrative makes for itself.[10] Controversy over Jn's distinctive Christology was probably the chief reason the author sought credibility. This effort further suggests that one of the major purposes of the FG was to present a corrective view of Jesus.

The narrator from his retrospective stance combines scripture with memory but also uses the historic present tense to convey immediacy—to provide a supremely authoritative interpretation of Jesus' words. Using Jesus' repeated references to his origin and destiny in his farewell speech, the author presents his significance for the author's own time. Indeed, key terms in that discourse like "hour," "glorify," "spirit," and "out of the synagogue" are introduced in early chapters as a way to link up the entire Gospel with Jesus' death. "What Jesus says, and the gospel as a whole, represents a massive, daring re-interpretation of Jesus,"[11] always from the life situation of the Johannine community.

Unlike Schnackenburg and von Wahlde, Culpepper thinks it is impossible to tell when Jesus or John the Baptist stops speaking in chapter 3 and when or if the narrator speaks (3:13–21 or 16–21 and 3:31–36).[12] That for him is not a matter of great consequence, since all three reflect the author's speech patterns and point of view.

The closest Culpepper comes to discussing Jn's composition history is to say that an examination of 19:35 and 21:24–25 may throw some light on it.[13] There are probably three persons involved: the implied author, the BD, and the narrator. Using the common technique of storytellers known as framing, the narrator employs the convention "we" in 1:14, 16 and again at 21:24, addressing the hearers directly in what is generally taken to be the original conclusion of the Gospel: "to help you believe…that you may have life in his name" (20:31). But another commonly used device employed to give the sense of an ending is the death of the person representing the dominant authorial point of view. Thus, there is 21:23, where the BD's death is implied. This yields a narrator (in another vocabulary, the final redactor) who has idealized a historical figure as the "disciple whom Jesus loved," making him in fact the implied author, that is, the literary image of the real person who did the writing, a second or superior self. This is the one who knows Jesus intimately and can interpret him reliably. His witness, in a word, is true (19:35; 21:24). This solution transcends the historical question of who contributed what to the final text by discovering from the text itself the narrator's view of the literary process.

Culpepper's chapter on plot development in Jn with its application of the central features' sequence, causality, unity, and affective power of the narrative takes the reader deeply into the text. Jesus is first introduced as the revealer of the Father (1:18) and authorizer of the children of God (v. 12), who then slowly "achieves his goals while his fortune apparently changes for the worse."[14] The plot develops as Jesus' identity comes to be recognized and fails to gain recognition. The suspense is provided by this question: Will successive characters in the Gospel acknowledge him for who he is and thereby receive eternal life? The same story is repeated over and over. The discourses slow down the action yet provide interpretive interludes that shed light on it. Chapter 12 is the bridge from the successive recognitions or rejections of Jesus to his capture. Following it he experiences the agony of accepting his death (vv. 27–28), through which the name of the Father will be glorified and he will draw us to himself (vv. 27–32). The characters Nicodemus, the disciples, the various beneficiaries of Jesus' signs, and Pilate are the subject of one of

Culpepper's chapters; the commentary implicit in the use of mis-understanding, irony, and conscious symbolism, of another. His study ends by convincing the reader that the FG is a sophisticated example of the narrative art. As to its authorial audience or intended readership, believers in Jesus seem clearly to be the targeted group rather than Jews who do not believe in him or Samaritans or Gentiles. The believers are expected to know most of the story characters and its general outlines but not about the BD, Lazarus, Nicodemus, or Annas and Caiaphas. A familiarity with Jewish festivals is assumed—not, however, specific places in the land of Israel or Jewish customs. A broader readership was evidently envisioned at a later stage than the one originally intended. As to the overall purpose of the Gospel, it has to be authentic faith in Jesus, the revealer of God, as contrasted with inauthentic faith.

Studies in the Johannine Irony

One expansion and elaboration of an aspect of Culpepper's literary inquiry, namely, Jn's use of irony, has been provided by his student **Paul D. Duke.** Duke understands irony to be a Hellenistic technique employed to treat themes of primarily Jewish concern. In it, a subtle literary choice is being offered to the first hearers of Jn. The choice is between the surface level of meaning and an alternative level. This alternative always provides a higher estimation of Jesus than the one that appears on the surface. It is, in a word, christological. "The numerous ironic silences of the Gospel and its rich suggestiveness of language seem to presuppose an audience at least partially conditioned to this mode of expression."[15] In Duke's view the technique is less a product of Jewish writings (Esther, Tobit) than of the fifth-century BC Greek tragedies of Sophocles and Euripides as presaged by Homer. The devices basic to Jn's thought assume a bi-level, literary vision, a duality that invites the hearer from one level of comprehension to

another. Among the devices are metaphor, double meaning, mis-
understanding, and ironic speech proper.

Metaphor is easy to recognize if not always to understand:
for example, the "I AM" sayings, "living water," Jesus' going
where he cannot be found, the "grain of wheat [that must] die."
The two levels of meaning are deeply identified. In metaphor they
invite extension, connection, and exploration, whereas in irony
they are in opposition. The Johannine double meanings, for their
part, convey deliberate ambiguity: One reality is used figuratively
to illumine another. Among them are "going up [to the feast]," 7:8;
"from above," a better rendering of *anōthen* than "anew," 3:3, 7;
"it is expedient for you," 11:50, and "it is to your advantage," 16:7,
the same Greek verb; "to die for," 11:50–51; 18:14; "to lift/be
lifted up," 3:14; 8:28; 12:32, 34; and "it is finished/completed,"
19:30. In every case—and there are others besides these—speakers say more than they realize or else the narrator hints at or leaves
open the possibility of a higher level of meaning. The Johannine
misunderstandings are well known: those of Nicodemus, the
Samaritan woman, the crowd that experienced the miracle of the
loaves, the disciples who took Lazarus's "sleep" for death, and
Martha, who confused resurrection on the last day with the "life"
Jesus came to give. In all such cases, those who hear the FG are
summoned to a stance superior to that of the characters and are
thereby drawn into a circle of enlightenment.

As to the ironies of the Gospel properly so called, they are
any patterns of speech that imply or assume an intimacy between
the author and at least a portion of the audience. This bond conveys to the hearer how to interpret what follows. Sometimes
Johannine irony is used as a weapon in controversy, the victims
being any persons who presume to have more knowledge ("the
Jews"), more privilege (Peter), or more power (Pilate) than they
do. Outstanding examples are false claims to know Jesus' origins
(6:42; 7:27, 41b–42, 52b) and unconscious testimonies to him
(11:48; 12:19; 18:33, 39). But whether used as mockery, witness,
or inspiration, Jn's irony offers "constant silent invitations

[intended] 'to persuade believers to become Christians' [François Vouga]."[16]

Gail O'Day in a follow-up literary study observes that Bultmann was concerned with the mere fact that Jesus was the revealer of God *(kḗrygma)* and Käsemann overmuch with the content or *what* of his revelation *(dogma)*. She proceeds to show that the *how* of Jesus' revelation is of primary importance to Jn.[17] That accounts for the subtitle of her study—*Narrative Mode and Theological Claim*—since for her the FG makes its theological claims through the way it tells its story. She too thinks that irony in Jn, which she defines after Muecke as "some form of perceptible contradiction, disparity, incongruity or anomaly,"[18] supplies the key. In support of her contention she analyzes Jn 4:4–42 at greatest length. There she discovers that Jn's principal means of engaging the reader in the Jacob's well story is irony. The chapter employs contrasts and disparities showing two narrative levels, often occurring simultaneously, that are at odds. Repetition also occurs in which the words of one character are picked up and used by another to give them new meaning (e.g. "give me a drink," v. 7; "give me this water," v. 15). There are ironic contrasts between what is anticipated and what is said (vv. 17 and 18). The opaqueness of the woman or the disciples as to what is going on indicates to hearers that they should do more or other than the characters do, even though these be disciples or favored persons like the woman to whom a revelation is made. In brief, O'Day's point is that, as to proclamation or content, ch. 4 does not advance the hearers' knowledge over what they have been told in the prologue. Only the *narrative mode* through which a *theological claim* is made, both in this chapter and throughout, shows the glory of God revealed in the person of Jesus. Everything in the FG leads to the cross through "a total register ... of narrative possibilities[:] images, metaphors, and stories."[19] Amos Wilder is further quoted as saying: "We will not behold his glory, glory as of the only Son of the Father" (1:14) until we "allow the Fourth Gospel's narrative embodiment of Jesus to have its full say."[20]

The Passion Story as Part of the Whole Gospel:
A Human Jesus Crucified

Chapters 18–20 are just as important to the plot of John's Gospel for **G. C. Nicholson** as for O'Day. Both hold this in opposition to Ernst Käsemann, who thinks the Gospel effectively over when Jesus reports back to the Father in ch. 17.[21] The New Zealand scholar examines the three "lifting up" sayings of Jn (3:14; 8:28; 12:32ff.) in the total context of its ascent/descent or above/below motif and discovers that the crucifixion section is no "mere postscript" (Käsemann). It was not the gospel tradition of a passion narrative, already in place, that required John to do likewise. A crucifixion account was essential to his plot. In it Jesus came to "his own," becoming there a stranger to all but a few who believed in him and understood that he had to return above. The community "beheld his glory" (1:14) through understanding the death of Jesus in the context of his movement back to the Father. The meaning of the events of the passion is withheld from them until they receive the message of his need to ascend (20:17). Only then do they receive the Spirit from the risen Jesus (vv. 19–23). The point Jn makes of the passion narrative is that the crucifixion is not an ignominious death but a return to glory. Nicholson thinks that the reality of the human nature of the earthly Jesus, now glorified, "is not discussed…because it was not an issue" for John or his community.[22] It is a major issue for Käsemann, however, who holds that Jn's Christology of glory is "naively docetic" because his Jesus is always on the side of God. He is never portrayed as a real, suffering, finite human being.

Marianne Meye Thompson methodically takes Käsemann on, and all others who held this view before him (Baur, Wrede, Wetter, Hirsch). Her study is called *The Humanity of Jesus in the Fourth Gospel*.[23] She is likewise convinced that Bultmann is wrong to understand Jesus' humanity *(sarx)*—the polar opposite of his divinity that hides the latter from view—to be not an antidocetic device but a paradox, an offense, that must be overcome by faith.

Luise Schottroff is thought to be equally wrong in holding that although Jesus was fully human, this fact is irrelevant for faith. Schottroff thinks the FG denies that *any* material reality is relevant, not only the flesh of the revealer, for "the flesh profits nothing" (6:63). Thompson's response to all three is an exhaustive scrutiny of Jesus' human origins, the materiality of his signs, and the death of Jesus in Jn. She finds this Gospel neither docetic nor antidocetic. Jn affirmed Jesus' divine identity in the strongest possible terms, but for him that did not obliterate his humanity. His human status "does not finally limit or *define* him; nevertheless, his uniqueness or *un*likeness does not efface his humanity."[24]

Initial Explorations of the Sociological Setting of Jn

David Rensberger in his *Johannine Faith and Liberating Community*[25] joins the many who think that a particularly powerful theologian and literary artist recast certain, possibly oral traditions, perhaps even his own homilies, in a situation of conflict, crisis, and alienation.[26] The evangelist's purpose in stories like those of Nicodemus (ch. 3) and the blind man (ch. 9) is to show that confessing "faith in Jesus in the full Johannine sense requires a break with rival forms of Jewish belief."[27] A succession of borderline groups in the social environment of the Jn community are addressed: Jews who do not believe in Jesus (2:14–22); the secret Christian Jews (2:23–3:21); the followers of John the Baptist (3:22–26); finally, the Samaritans.[28] None of this hypothesizing is new but it is put forward with brevity and persuasiveness. Rensberger places Nicodemus among the Jewish rulers who were among the cryptobelievers in the divinely sent teacher Jesus, but who did not possess the faith adequate to a full and open confession.[29] This Pharisee is seen as a communal symbolic figure because he and Jesus both use the plural of direct address (3:2, 7, 11–12).

Rensberger's special contribution is his insistence on the cor-
porate nature of belief in the FG, neither individualist nor "spiritual." In addition he sees baptism "from above" and eating Jesus'
flesh and drinking his blood as symbols of the community's Christology, which serve as thresholds or limits of membership. He
exegetes the pertinent pericopes carefully (3:5; 3:22—4:1;
6:51c–58) to show that any theory of interpolated passages betraying a sacramental outlook is at odds with the author's conviction
about symbol as the vehicle of faith. Removing the disputed
eucharistic passage of ch. 6 above, for example, would make prob-
lematic why the disciples should have departed after the "hard"
words of vv. 60–71. The elimination would further require that the
phrase "the flesh is no benefit" be an interpolation responding to
an interpolation.[30] The "abiding" in Jesus of 6:56 by eating and
drinking him (cf. 14:20 and "even more strongly" 15:4–7) suggests that the "life" that follows results from maintaining the
Johannine christological confession.[31] Mutual love is communal
solidarity against a hostile world that either does not believe in
Jesus or believes otherwise in him.

Rensberger shows how Jn uses the trial scene before Pilate
to assert the power of Israel's God, and the one sent by God, over
the world's certainties. He finds in it, contrary to the usual asser-
tion of the evangelist's apologetic concern, a fine disregard of
confrontation with Rome. All that has preceded in his study leads
to a chapter relating certain interests important to Jn to the contemporary problems of the liberation of black people, women, the
poor, and other oppressed groups. The FG at first appears the least
promising of the four for the purpose because it lacks Jesus' radical social and economic pronouncements. Rensburger sees in the
Gospel, however, the product of a religiously oppressed community that had, at the same time, held on to a form of anti-Roman
Jewish messianism. He views baptism in Jn (ch. 3) as a dangerous
social relocation for those who make the change and Johannine
Christology as presenting a Jesus for the oppressed because of the
community's perception of itself in that role. Accepting baptism

on the terms of Johannine faith in Jesus meant a realignment of the ruler class of teachers with "the accursed," a band of radicals, fanatics "who did not know the law" (7:49)—in brief, a move from the role of persecutors to persecuted."[32]

Such a reading of the FG finds support in the seminal contribution of **Wayne Meeks,** perhaps the most frequently cited article of the past two decades, which sees in Jn's Jesus an alien, a stranger, "from above," "not of this world."[33] Jn's "sectarianism" is taken by Rensberger to mean a minority counterculture consciously opposed to much of the status quo in its environment. This makes it a serviceable paradigm for all social situations where a faith commitment underlies resistance to an oppressive majority. The exegete is at pains to point out that nothing of the classical "spiritual" interpretation of the FG is denied, only that besides an individual reading of the experience of believers a social one is demanded by the nature and origin of this Gospel.[34]

Depending equally, or more so, on Meeks's interpretation of the Johannine Jesus as a sojourner visiting from heaven, and on anthropologist Mary Douglas's group and grid categories to plot relationships in society, **Jerome Neyrey** views the FG not so much literarily as sociologically, although one footnote on "point of view" shows his familiarity with some leading studies of narrative.[35] His main concern is to discover the self-image of the community that produced the Gospel in its own time and place. Assuming the writing to be a mirror of the struggles of the community and omitting all overt reference to the historicity of events in Jesus' life, Neyrey first devotes four chapters to an exegesis of the Johannine presentation of Jesus as equal to God (5:18; 10:33; 8:24, 28, 58, where "I AM" has no predicate nominative), but not of this world (17:5, 14, 16, 24). Chapters 5, 8, 10, and 11 receive the bulk of attention. The affirmations of Jesus' divinity in 1:1–18 and 20:28 are not explored, Neyrey says, in part because they have been dealt with so frequently, but also because the above four chapters say so much more about Jesus' status and powers as a figure equal to God (Jn's "high christology"). These powers are chiefly two, the power to create (see 5:19–20, with emphasis on "whatever" and "all," and 5:26) and the power to raise the dead and judge them on the last day (5:21–29). Neyrey finds the latter pericope functioning as a "characteristic Johannine topic sentence." It serves as the agenda for developing the "new eschatological predications made of Jesus in John 8, 10, 11."[36] Verses 17–29 of chapter 5 of themselves provide "convincing proof" that they "reflect a later redaction of 5:10–16, 30–47," focusing on a Johannine high Christology.[37] They belong to the same period as the addition of 1:1–18 and 20:28 to the FG, all featuring Jesus' equality with God.[38]

Verses 12–20 of chapter 8 reflect an earlier tradition, which depicts Jesus as a plaintiff "defending his actions on the Sabbath against hostile Jews"; vv. 21–30, however, portray him as a judge speaking only as the Father has taught him, vv. 49–50 as one who deserves honor equal to God's, and vv. 51–53 as the giver of postmortem life.[39] The three passages are taken to be the result of later redactional activity, a process that Neyrey will find operative in two stages in ch. 11.

But first, in ch. 10, verses 1–27 contain Jesus' basic parables, the popular judgment on him, and the forensic defense of his claims. These are thought to represent "the replacement stage" of composition, which names him the authentic successor of all the Jewish ritual and inauthentic shepherding that preceded him. Verses 28–30, prepared for by 17–18, represent new claims: having life in himself and being equal to God. Both are the result of later redactive development. The two stages of editing in the ch. 11 Lazarus story—at base, a Synoptic-like account of a resuscitation miracle—were, first, the adjustment required to meet "the death of Jesus' beloved disciple" (meaning Lazarus), whom some under the influence of texts like 11:26 had thought deathless ("Whoever lives and believes in me shall never die"; see also 8:52), and "still another redaction in which Jesus' eschatological power over death was demonstrated (11:4, 25)."[40]

These citations should convey adequately Neyrey's technique in what he calls "traditional methods of exegesis." Anything that describes Jesus as more than the Messiah, a prophet, or an agent of God's power was added in a second or middle stage. Attribution to him of the exclusively divine powers of creation and eschatological judgment were more likely proper to a third stage. Primary were those presentations of Jesus that propagated the Christian mission, the middle stage being that which showed him replacing the Jewish patriarchs, rites, and cultures. The University of Notre Dame exegete simply cites the researches of those who have theorized on sources in Jn without calling upon their contributions. His reconstructions are, practically speaking, entirely his own. The principle is simple. A new redaction is posited for each perceived set of claims for Jesus' powers and, at the end, an editing in a corrective spirit.

This prepares the reader for the second of two parts in *An Ideology of Revolt,* "Not of This World: Christology in Social Science Perspective." In the categories of Mary Douglas, when a "group" conforms to society's definitions, classifications, and evaluations, it is said to be "strong," but increasingly weaker as societal pressure on the group decreases. "Low grid" rising to "high" is the description of the socially constrained adherence normally given by a group's members to a prevailing symbol system.[41] Thus, the Johannine church in its early stages would have viewed Jesus as a member of the Jewish covenant community (see Jn 17:3; 1:45; 5:39; 7:40–44, 52), a "strong group" situation, but then it remembered the way he challenged structured life in Israel—a "low-grid" situation regarding Sabbath observance and the like.[42] Such is the first stage of the Gospel's composition, which Neyrey labels the time of "missionary propaganda." In stage two, called "replacement," Jesus is presented as true temple, cult, and feast at the center of a community that is increasingly elitist. Stage three is the period of "high Christology" (weak group/low grid) in which spirit is celebrated over matter (6:63), individual personality takes over from group (branches attached

to the vine are given as an example of immediate access to Jesus),
no ritual behavior is prescribed (again, 6:63), and sin "becomes a
matter of personal and interior decision" (8:24; see 13:8).[43]

The Life-Setting of the Fourth Gospel:
From Brown to Neyrey

It was Raymond E. Brown who set the terms for reconstruct-
ing the life of the Johannine church in his deceptively simple *The
Community of the Beloved Disciple,* originally papers—some of
them presidential addresses—before learned societies.[44] He plotted
the tensions he discerned in the text of the FG, which were chiefly
with the community's neighboring Jewish population and other
believers in Jesus over the matter of its high Christology. A deeper
exploration of the subsequent course of community events is found
in his Doubleday Anchor commentary on the letters.[45]

Neyrey identifies the introduction of Mary Douglas's
anthropological model into Judaic studies with a book of Jacob
Neusner on purity in ancient Judaism (1975). **Bruce Malina,**
however, seems to be the pioneer in adapting her work to New
Testament studies.[46] Neyrey, having done a few preliminary articles, turns himself over thoroughly to her method of inquiry. He
sees the dichotomous patterns in Jn of heaven vs. earth, spirit vs.
flesh, from above vs. from below, and not of this world vs. of this
world as boundary-setting categories between the followers of
Jesus and the synagogue and even some apostolic-age Christians.
(The beloved disciple vs. Peter figures in the same way.)[47] In
stages one and two, respectively the period of signs and the period
of replacement, the Johannine community's reforming intent
brought it into contact with the synagogue on terms of competi-
tion and conflict. First the Christians' claims needed defending,
then true rites had to replace obsolete or false ones; initially the
criteria for leadership were in need of reform, then the reality of
ritual. In stage three, the period of high Christology, no value is

seen in earth or flesh, only heaven and spirit. "The telltale evidence of this is 6:63 and 8:23, in which all value is placed not in material rites or in anything fleshly, earthly, or material, but in spirit alone."[48] Reform is deserted for revolt against all former structures, criteria, and systems. Expulsion from the synagogue (9:22; 12:42) led to the Jn group's physical relocation but also to a new, cosmological placement "above," "not of this world." These recurring changes of location and value were symbolized by the pairing of spirit over matter, flesh, and body. Confessing Jesus as "equal to God" shares the posture of revolt against all systems, whether of the synagogue or the apostolic churches. The triumph of spirit over matter is complete.

Nowhere does Neyrey declare the FG in its final form a Gnostic document, nor does he claim Ernst Käsemann's parentage for his theorizing.[49] It is as if Mary Douglas's vocabulary of purity and liminality, strong/weak bodily control replicating strong/weak social control, and sin as corrupting pollutant or as a matter of personal, interior decision seeks perfect expression and finds it in the FG. As with John A. T. Robinson's germ of an idea, a fruitful theory of limited application seems to have taken control of the Gospel in its three stages, previously arrived at. Again and again a certain few texts are called on to support a predetermined structure.

Okure's Contextual Method:
Successive Missions of the Son and the Disciples

A study done by a Nigerian exegete does not so much challenge the assumption of Neyrey and others that each redaction of the Gospel originated with meeting the special needs of the community addressed, as let the FG dictate its own hermeneutical principles, paying attention to what is being said in the final text, *how,* and, speculatively, *why.*[50] **Teresa Okure** calls her method of study "contextual," contrasting it with stopping at a search for

sources and successive editings but not ruling out dialogue with
such theories of composition. By "contextual" she means a combination of rhetorical and literary analysis in the quest for theological meaning, viewed from the standpoint of the evangelist
(final author) and what is presumed to be his intended audience.[51]
One passage of the canonical text will thus be used to highlight
another, part speaking to part. The dialectic going on among passages in the FG is taken to be its intended rhetorical mode (as
stressed by Schnackenburg, Brown, Dodd, and others), not a matter of contradictions unresolved by the editing process. The contextual method presupposes a reasonably consistent use of terms
by Jn and so looks for meaning in disputed passages by recourse
to usage in both the immediate context and other parts of the
Gospel (as with "to labor," "to speak [her] say-so," and "to testify" in Jn 4, which the book chooses for exegetical treatment, at
vv. 6, 26, 30, 38, 42). This "listening approach" to the various levels of Johannine rhetoric is by no means a historicism, although it
incorporates historical meaning synchronically with the literary
and the theological.[52] The study seeks, overall, to offer a unified
interpretation of the evangelist's conception of mission, as indicated by the title.

Much contemporary scholarship in the German and
Romance languages has confined the term *mission* (the word is
the same in the two language groups) to bringing the gospel to
unbelievers in the erroneously termed third world, while favoring
sending for its occurrence in Jn. Okure's major thesis is that mission properly describes the sending of the Son by the Father and
the Son's sending of the disciples to proclaim him Christ and Son
of God to believers and any who may come to believe. She is
aware of the propriety of rendering *pempein* and *apostellein* by
"send" but finds much of modern scholarship insensitive to the
missionary dialectic in Jn between the audience and the one sent
that reaches its climax in 20:30–31. That is an explicit statement
of the FG's purpose in evangelistic terms. Okure wants the
Gospel to be seen in that way, since for her these are the only

terms on which the evangelist presents it. Few experts in Jn today
see it as a missionary tract directed to Jews or Gentiles. Most find
it written for a believing community, some holding for Samaritans as a secondary audience. The question is: Do the evident
apologetic, polemic, and parenetic motifs in Jn disqualify it as
having a missionary purpose, a term redolent in today's world of
pagan populations?

There is widespread agreement that the Johannine community had a missionary interest in its first stages. Many think, however, that this concern lost out in a community that was in its final
stages closed, sectarian, and inward-looking, delivering polemic
tirades against its enemies. Okure holds that these views, coupled
with those that see a primarily soteriological or eschatological
significance in the sending of the Son, tend to obscure the evangelist's understanding of mission. Only this, she thinks, accounts for
the Gospel's constant choice of Jesus' interaction with his audience in the form of dialogues, in which the characters are never
mere foils, and discourses. In both he is the one sent and the
sender. His mission from the Father is primary and is paralleled
by his sending his friends on the identical mission, "that you may
believe...and that believing you may have life..." The mission of
the Paraclete is scarcely dealt with in this study (only on p. 32).
The Holy Spirit as a witness to Jesus (along with the Baptist)
fares only slightly better.

Three long chapters are devoted to an exegesis of Jn 4:1–42.
A survey of authors reveals that, whatever is thought of the origins
of vv. 31–38 in the text, most start with the understanding that mission in the passage refers only or primarily to the post-Easter
activity of the disciples. Okure counters with the working hypothesis that all of vv. 1–42 deals with Jesus' mission from the Father
but from three different perspectives. These are the outlook of the
nonbelieving woman (1–26 [27], the *narratio*), the disciples,
whom Jesus instructs in the nature of their involvement in mission
(31–38, the *expositio*), and the normative character of Jesus' mission based as it is on the relationship between the missionaries and

those they bring to faith in Jesus (28–30; 39–42, the *demonstratio*). The structural relationship of parts may be compared to that of a *sēmeion* and its explanatory discourse.

Another chapter analyzes vv. 7–26 for the relation of the themes of salvation as God's gift for the asking and the identity of Jesus as the Christ appointed by God to dispense it; the rhetorical devices employed (philosophic persuasion rather than forensic attack, irony); and the passage's missionary features, chiefly Jesus' manner and method of approach to the woman, his respect for her as a person rather than as a member of a hostile group, and her being led to discovery of what "the gift of God" might mean. The "consequential argument" of vv. 31–42 that follows on the "thesis" of 1–26 shows Jesus as the one who alone sows with the Father in a "work" that is the new world order brought about by his mission. The eschaton is the new time order in which this new world order operates. In Jn it is a reality that spans both the sowing and the harvesting phases of the "work." Johannine eschatology is essentially realized eschatology, in Jesus' mission realized both in believers (as life) and in unbelievers (as judgment).

The division of the pericope into its three main parts (vv. 7–26; 27, 31–38; 28–30, 39–42) reveals three distinct moments in the missionary enterprise but should not mask the literary and thematic unity of 4:1–42. Essential to the missionary undertaking is the interaction between the one sent and his audience, which has as its purpose to evoke a faith response to the divine agent and his message. Mutual exchange between Jesus and his dialogue partners seems threatened by the double entendre in which Jesus understands a reality above nature to be in question when his partner is operating at the level of nature. But the audience has not been left behind by this literary technique. A divine being striding the earth has not been inserted, leaving the revealer and his message as all that matters (Wrede, Bultmann, Käsemann). Instead, the effort is made to use language meaningful to the audience to convey realities in the heavenly realm that are within their grasp.[53] Almost all of the narrative sections and asides in this chapter deal with the different situations of conflict, missionary and social, that underlie it and relate to the situation of the evangelist and his audience.

It is perhaps erroneous to classify Okure's study as literary on a par with those of Culpepper, Duke, and O'Day. Like Thompson's and those in the chapter to follow, it might better be viewed as the treatment of a single Johannine theme. Similarly, Neyrey's work is concerned with one thing, the practical effects in the community of the increasingly heightened Christology. Yet all six research pieces have in common a new awareness of the literary product, that is, the text we have in hand, as it relates to the circumstances in the life of the community that begot it.

The Spirit in Jn as God's Power at Work
in Jesus/the Risen Christ

Such a work is **Gary Burge**'s dissertation presented to the University of Aberdeen under the supervision of Professor I. Howard Marshall.[54] Its absorption in the questions of the Paraclete (four times in Jn), the Spirit of truth (three times), and more broadly the Spirit (eleven times with the article, seven without; Holy Spirit, without the article twice, with once) at first gives the impression that this will be yet another word study providing unavoidable conclusions in academic form. It proves to be much more encompassing and richer than that. The Paraclete problem is tackled first (see 14:16, 26; 15:26; 16:7; 1 Jn 2:1). The traditional meaning of the word in its few pre- and extra-Christian usages is "intercessor" or "helper," only rarely "legal advocate." Jn employs it, not entirely to describe a replacement figure for the glorified Christ (who continues to be present to the disciples), but as one through whom Christ speaks as he directs the Paraclete's revealing activity. In the era of the church the Paraclete is a forensic or "juridical Spirit…giving evidence before the world [in the form of] unique revelations. As Christ was on trial and revealed the Father, so too the disciples (and the Paraclete) were on trial, and in their witness they glorified and revealed Christ."[55] Jesus' glorification alone made the Spirit available (2:39; 19:30, 34).

Burge cites favorably and at length two Catholic scholars in this connection. **F. Porsch**[56] and **I. de la Potterie.**[57] Porsch believes that "revelation—the close connection between Spirit and word—is John's overarching message."[58] Jn 6:63 is a pivotal text for him. "From the fact that Jesus gives the Spirit…it is established that he speaks God's words.…*The giving of the Spirit and the speaking of the word of God* are not two different acts…but are…as a single event. Since Jesus speaks the words of God or reveals *(lalei)* he also gives the Spirit at the same time."[59] Porsch sees in 3:34, too, Jesus as the giver of the Spirit in speaking God's words.

The primacy of the word is indeed central to Johannine pneumatology, Burge concedes, but he thinks that the emphasis of Jn on *pneuma* as achieving the unique anointing of the Messiah is the Gospel's greater concern (Jn 1:32, 33, based on Is 42:1). The christological concentration of Jn's pneumatology is assured whether revelation or anointing takes precedence, but Burge finds the indwelling of the Spirit that follows Jesus' anointing paramount. Examining the part the Spirit plays in Jesus' ministry in Jn, Burge discovers it to be God's dynamic, mysterious power working in him, before his exaltation especially, but also after it, "Jesus living powerfully within the community and continuing his work among his followers."[60] In the account of Jesus' baptism (1:29–34), John's experience of the Spirit is described but his baptizing Jesus is not mentioned.[61] The Spirit's empowering of Jesus (vv. 32, 33) is most important for Jn. The dove—a tradition deriving, Burge thinks, from Is 11:2 (where the spirit of the Lord rests on the shoot from Jesse's stump)—confirms Jesus as God's chosen one (v. 34).

Once anointed by the Spirit, the Johannine Christ is not Spirit-impelled to exorcise or perform miracles, as in the Synoptics. The power he has comes from God, but the signs he performs reveal not his power but his glory. The miracles are intensely christological in intent. As part of this Spirit Christology, "Jesus speaks the words of God ([3]:34a) by virtue of his unlimited anointing in the Spirit....The Spirit is one gift among many (["all things"] 3:35) that Jesus has in full....The Spirit which Jesus immeasurably has will manifest itself in the words he speaks."[62] Jesus has been sent by God to reveal the Father whose gift of the Spirit certifies his revelation. The seal on Jesus of 6:27 is the Spirit, "not a power impulsively resident in Jesus but an attribute of his own person."[63] As Jesus distributes the water alive within him (7:37–38; cf. 4:14), Jn makes clear that this water is Spirit to be dispensed only through the cross (7:39; see 19:34). By the Spirit Jesus is constituted the new temple (2:18–19) from which living waters will flow (see Ez 47:1; Zech 14:8).

"Jesus is the visible presence of the Father, and the life and being of Jesus waiting to be poured forth into the world is the Spirit."[64] This presence is manifested in Jesus' lifetime through his words, which are Spirit and life (6:63). Union with Jesus is depicted in Jn as first appropriating, then remaining in, his word (5:24; 8:51; 14:23; 17:6). Jn's Christology of sonship is formed on a prophetic model (see 4:19; 9:17). Jesus is an agent sent by God (sixteen times) but, more than that, he is the Moses-like prophet of the final days (Dt 18:17; cf. Jn 6:14; 7:40). He has manifested God's name (17:6; cf. Ex 3:13–14), his words are equal to scripture (8:28; 17:8), but, most importantly, a centrality is claimed for him that Israel claimed for Torah (see 5:39–40, 46–47). Word, prophet, and Spirit are brought together in Johannine Christology so that it is indistinguishably a pneumatology, in ultimate purpose revelatory of God.

Jn considers 20:22 (Jesus' breathing of the Spirit on his disciples) to be the climax of the relation between them, the fulfillment of their expectation so carefully developed in the farewell discourses. In the two next-to-last chapters (19–20) Jn brings together the death, resurrection, ascension, and anointing of Jesus in the single event of his glorification, his "hour." The Spirit has been released through the cross. Now Christ and the Spirit must never be separated. The Father bestows the Spirit as an effective encounter with Jesus. The parousia has not been spiritualized, as is so often said. Rather, the Spirit—eternal life (it is one and the same)—now dwells within.[65]

Burge, unlike Bultmann and Protestant scholarship generally, does not think that the preredacted Jn has no place for sacraments. Worship of the Father "in Spirit" (4:23) is for him not a rejection of ritualism and ceremony. It is a requirement that all such action refer to a power from God mediated by Christ. This worship is directed toward the flesh and blood of Jesus; the Spirit he supplies will empower it.[66] The community knows Christ in power, Christ in the Spirit. Its anointing with the Spirit means that its members must be on guard against any celebration of baptism or Eucharist that does not deepen their experience and knowledge of the Spirit, or instill in the community a sense of unity and love. Worship "in truth" (4:23) *may* mean that which is genuine or grounded in reality but is more likely to be an anticipation of the wisdom Christology that sees Christ as the truth (14:6).

Just as Jesus is sent by God, so he sends the Spirit from the Father in a mission identical with that of the disciples acting as the church. The Paraclete sustains the presence of Jesus and effectively enables the church to complete the revealing work of Christ. The Paraclete is advocate and witness to a church enduring persecution, enabling it to speak prophetically. In discussing the Johannine epistles in a brief coda, Burge first maintains that charism is not set entirely in opposition to tradition.[67] He opposes the view of Käsemann and Bornkamm that the epistles represent entrenchment as opposed to expansion, identifying himself with Brown's position that the community required adjustment to a crisis in pneumatology and revelation. Despite this, he accepts their vocabulary of pneumatic vitality vs. catholicism, prophecy vs. tradition. On the basis of the epistolary literature, the missing mean between the extremes would seem to be adhering to the dialectic between anamnesis and inspiration. The tragic opposite of "catholicism" appears to have been a departing from the dialectic into communities that opted for the guidance of the Spirit apart from the remembered tradition.

Jesus on Trial in Jn over Fidelity to Torah

The year 1975 saw the appearance of a lengthy portion of a dissertation by a Canadian diocesan priest entitled *The Law in the Fourth Gospel.*[68] **Severino Pancaro** submitted it to the Münster faculty, writing under the direction of Joachim Gnilka. The subtitle, *The Torah and the Gospel, Moses and Jesus, Judaism and Christianity According to John,* gives some indication of the explicit character of its 571 pages. Viewing Jn as a report on the life and faith of a specific community, probably ethnically Jewish in a much larger Jewish milieu, Pancaro explores carefully the passages that show Jesus charged with being a violator of the Sabbath and of the Law; with being a sinner (5:16, 18; 9:16, 24); a blasphemer (5:17–18; 8:58; 10:24–38); a false teacher who leads people astray (7:14–18, 45–49; 9:24–34; 18:19–24); and an enemy of the Jewish people (11:47–52). This succession of Torah challenges gives the entire Gospel a juridical character, making a hearing before Caiaphas the high priest needless (because the outcome was predetermined, 11:49–52; but see 18:24, 28). Jesus cannot be right in the face of these charges, from the point of view of his adversaries at law, "the Jews," and he cannot be wrong from the standpoint of the believing community. The opposition to him does not have the faith required to see in him someone "from God" who must work even as his Father works, who does not blaspheme when he claims to be the Son of God or equal to God, who leads no one astray but only along the same path as Moses. Jesus summons successive witnesses on his behalf: the Baptizer, his works, the revelation made to Israel, the scriptures. None of these will do, for as Jonathan Swift once said of embattled neighbors trading compliments over a back fence, they were arguing from different premises. The disciples of Jesus cannot view anything ever again

as do those who call themselves the disciples of Moses. The physical proximity of the two groups that would become synagogue
and church only heightens the drama. According to the Law, as
viewed from a certain perspective, Jesus has to die (19:7; cf.
18:32) and his followers have to be persecuted.

Pancaro asks: For whom would the apologetic tack taken by
Jn, that is, basing Jesus' authenticity on the Law in response to a
charge of total disregard of it, be meaningful? A Jewish audience
is his answer, in a struggle between the Johannine church made
up of "Jewish-Christians toward the end of the first century" and
" 'normative' Judaism."[69] *Ho nomos* in Jn for him always means
Torah, the Law, in its most comprehensive sense. "Your law"
(8:17) or "their law" (15:25) signals dissociation and distancing
but not opposition, except insofar as Jesus is above the Law
through having fulfilled it by his Father's will. In that sense his
followers too thought themselves beyond it because of their association with him. The Law retains all its value for Jesus and those
who believe in him, but they have given it the value he assigned
it, namely, of a witness to him. It is "your" or "their" law only in
the sense that it is the Law to which Jn's "Jews" appeal. To be of
the Johannine community with its christological faith is to know
what the scriptures mean and what Moses signified in the history
of the Jewish people. For Jn, all have a Christ meaning.

A much briefer book along the same lines appeared in England a year later by **A. E. Harvey** of King's College, London, and
St. Augustine's College, Canterbury.[70] He assumes that the author
of the FG possessed many of the same data from the tradition as
the Synoptics but opted to arrange them as a trial of Jesus, con-
ducted by Jewish authority and spread over his public life. Harvey suggests strongly that that was probably what happened in
Jesus' history. In a ten-page postscript he states that even if Jn
employed the literary form of a lawsuit or *ribh,* the episodes
reported are not rendered altogether unhistorical by that fact. This
is a considerable backing off from the intimation of the first 122
pages that all happened largely as described.

The FG must have been written for people who understood the legal procedures involved, Harvey thinks. Hence its audience was probably an intermediate culture between Jews and Gentiles that would have known the literary convention of argument as in a court of law like that found in Job and the prophets. "But again, the Jewishness of this Christian community may well not have been the most significant thing about it."[71] The author concludes he must leave open the question of whom the Gospel was written for, in part because of the textual uncertainty of John 20:31, "that you may continue to believe," *pisteuēte* (pres. subj.) or "come to believe," *pisteusēte* (aor. subj.). His final judgment is that it probably was not a missionary book but a book for believers to help them pass judgment, again and again, on the proposition now presented as an established fact that Jesus is the Christ, the Son of God.[72]

Harvey has no interest in the Roman trial that ended in a sentence of death. He assumes that Jesus was condemned by Jewish law on charges of Sabbath breaking and blasphemy and that the Roman prefect crucified him only because the Jews at that time could not, although "in reality it [viz., their citing their incapacity to pass capital sentence by Roman decree; see 18:31] may have been in the nature of an excuse."[73] Jewish legal authority, thwarted in its attempts to put Jesus to death, brought him to Pilate as a person seditious against the Roman state. But this was a totally implausible charge in light of the record about him.[74] St. Paul is cited at Gal 3:13 as part of the evidence that Jesus died on a Jewish charge and therefore accursed in the eyes of the Law. Presumably a civil condemnation that resulted in crucifixion would not have achieved this. Harvey cites those whom Jn calls on to testify that Jesus is the Son of God: John (1:19–20, 30–34; 3:28), Nathanael (1:49), the woman and the townspeople of Samaria (4:19, 42), and Simon Peter (6:69). To these are later added the Paraclete and the disciples (15:16–27). He makes much of the fact that Jewish law did not settle cases on evidence but on the testimony of witnesses, even a

single witness of high character. God, too, could be summoned to
witness the truth of what was said.[75]

Johannine Christology, Soteriology, and the Meaning of "Son of Man"

Two studies of substance that appeared in the mid-1970s are
the doctoral dissertations of **J. Terence Forestell,** a Canadian
Basilian,[76] and **Francis J. Moloney,** a Salesian of Don Bosco from
Australia.[77] The theses were defended, respectively, before the
Pontifical Biblical Commission and the University of Oxford.
Forestell observes that, while the most prominent theology of salvation in the NT sees Christ's death as expiatory for our sins,
restoring humanity thereby to the friendship of God (Synoptics,
Acts, Rom 3:25, but especially Heb), Jn avoids all language of sat-
isfaction or cult. The FG instead presents Jesus' death as integral
to the revelatory process in which God is self-manifested, bestow-
ing the divine life on all who believe in Christ (Jn 5:24). Only 1:29
could indicate the expiatory character of Jesus' death, but it is not
developed in Johannine fashion and may come from the eucharistic celebrations of the community.[78] The cross is the culminating
act in the revealing process, being the exaltation and glorification
of the Son of Man. The reception of the Word-become-flesh is life-
giving, but it is not merely the words or works of Jesus that produce this life; it is his very person as the manifestation of the
Father. The manifestation is complete when he lays down his life,
thereby revealing to believers God's life-giving love (6:51; 10:11;
11:50, 51; 15:13; 18:14). The preposition *hyper* ("for," "for the
sake of") occurs throughout but it describes the purpose of his
dying, not its cause, and never has sin as its object. This understanding of faith in the cross as saving is not reduction to Gnosis, a
mere doctrine about God, both because it is incarnational and
because the death is an integral part of the total revelation. This
should cause us to rethink the meaning of worship and sacrifice. In

Jn, Jesus' sacrifice has become a manifestation of God's word of love and a sanctification of Christ himself.

The Moloney study, done under the direction of Dr. F. Morna Hooker, establishes that "Son of Man" in Jn is always used of the human Jesus—from beginning to end of his career—and always in the third person. A Father–Son of Man relation never occurs. The Son of Man is the unique revealer of God because only he has ever come down from heaven (3:13; 6:62). As Son of Man he is a judge; he is lifted up in crucifixion; he is glorified on the cross. His hour has arrived as he goes to the cross (12:23, 34; 13:13; 19:5). When the Word became flesh, it became the Son of Man, not a convenient messianic term in Jn but an explanation of why Jesus is in the world: to reveal God. Jn has taken the term from the Christian tradition, which in turn derived it from Dan 7:13. There, one like a son of man comes before the Ancient of Days in company with the saints, to be given dominion and everlasting kingship. Jn presents Jesus under this title as the one by whom the world judges itself, depending on its acceptance or rejection of him.

"Son of Man" originated as a bit of idiomatic self-reference by Jesus for **Barnabas Lindars,** an Anglican Franciscan. It was not a title and has nothing of the apocalyptic Dan 7:13 about it. Jn derived it from the tradition of a passion saying (see 3:14) and used it to convey "the agent of the revelation which is disclosed in the cross."[79]

The book-length scholarship on the literary structure of Jn up to 1990 to be reported on ends here, with three exceptions. One treatment, necessarily hypothetical, will have to stand for the literally dozens of journal articles on the structure of individual pericopes that have appeared in the twenty years under review in this chapter. It is the work of a Swedish scholar, **Birger Olsson.**[80] Like many others, he is led by his careful text analysis to see in the Gospel a book written for believers, not a missionary tract. The basic message of the two passages he chooses for scrutiny is the way the people Israel of the latter covenant comes to birth from the former, with Samaritans included. Both the Cana story (2:1–11) and that of the Samaritan woman (4:1–42) are told on two levels, narrative and symbolic, with many allusions to biblical and deuterocanonical texts. Chapter 4 is multiply "screened," meaning composed of overlying strata. A basic *"ergon"* screen (the historical deed of Jesus) has had a "well" screen placed over it that draws on the narratives in Gen 29 and Ex 2:15ff. (Rachel and the seven daughters of the priest of Midian at their respective wells).

Ch. 4 was edited finally in such a way as to convey a sense of the gathering in of all the people of God. At the end of Olsson's laborious sleuthing into sources, seams, and first, second, and third levels of narration, he asks why the many who concur with him in seeing a narrative level overlaid by successive "screens" require a late date for the final composition. Why could it not all have developed rapidly, giving a much earlier date for Jn than is usually proposed? But this challenge is not the book's chief merit, which rather is to show how a text in the Gospel as it stands can be analyzed to reveal how it was constructed, and the internal language clues that suggest its levels of composition.

The second volume in summary is **Raymond E. Brown**'s 840-page commentary on the three letters of John — the first of them like Hebrews actually a treatise.[81] Their importance is that they identify a group of secessionists from the community who show the perils of taking the Christology and eschatology of the "GJohn" (his usage throughout) to extremes. Brown says there is no reason not to attribute authorship of all three epistles to the same person, although there is no way to prove that such was the case, and that they seem to come from a period after the evangelist completed his Gospel (ca. 90 for Brown) but before the final redactor's work (shortly after 100). Divisions in the community appear to have developed with the crystallizing of Johannine thought in the Gospel. This would account for the absence of polemic against *hoi Ioudaîoi* of 1 John. There is total absorption by the writer with the enemy within, namely, those "antichrists" and "liars" (1 Jn 2:18, 22) who do not hold that Jesus is the Christ who has come in the flesh (2 Jn 7). There is nothing in GJohn to require that second-century Christians go the way of what became orthodoxy *or* a variety of Gnostic heresies (apparently the path of the greater number). Neither can it be supposed that the epistles had only GJohn to go on; there surely was a more ample Johannine tradition (see Jn 21:25).

To follow Brown in his exhaustive treatment of a literature that covers only six pages in an ordinary Bible is to learn much more about the Gospel than a study confined to the epistles would yield. He generously suggests on an early page that the material in his introduction—which he proposes should be read both before and after the bulk of the book—and his notes after each pericope should provide sufficient aid to scholarly readers in arriving at other positions than those adopted in the extended "Comment" that follows the notes.

A textual study by **Ed L. Miller** in 1989 has as its subtitle *The Significance of John 1:3/4*.[82] The key to a correct translation of these verses is the proper punctuation missing from the earliest MSS. On it depends whether the *gégonen* of v. 3c refers to the *pánta* that "have appeared" of 3a or to "What has appeared in him." The author opts for placing a period after *oudè hén* ("not one thing"), the second option. His argument is that vv. 1c and 2 are an interpolation, leaving 1:1a–b and 3–5 as four strophes in parallel made up of 1a–b, 3a–b, 3c–d, and 5a–b. The five verses thus edited are thought to be a complete christological hymn added later to what now follows under the influence of 1 Jn 1–4.

Some Helpful Books for Students, Teachers, Preachers

Two popular presentations of Johannine research have been done by Professor **Pheme Perkins** of Boston College. The first of these was her *Gospel of St. John* in the Read and Pray series (Chicago, 1975), page-long comments on eighty eight passages for daily reflection over a three-month period. Her *The Gospel* *according to St. John: A Theological Commentary* (Chicago, 1978), 251 pages, followed it. Perkins devotes one chapter to each of the twenty-one chapters of the Gospel and provides comments on successive pericopes rather than individual verses. Part 1 is entitled "Calling Disciples" (chs. 1–4); 2, "Public Ministry" (5–12); 3, "Farewell Discourses" (13–17); and 4, "Crucifixion/ Resurrection: The Glorification of Jesus" (18–21). See also her *NJBC* commentary (1990).

Stephen S. Smalley, a Church of England scholar, produced in that same year *John: Evangelist and Interpreter* (Greenwood, 1978), 285 pages. He first gives a brief history of Johannine scholarship, then attempts to answer the questions concerning the Gospel: who, what, when, where, and why? Smalley opts for a third and final stage of composition at Ephesus by the apostle John, who is the beloved disciple. The treatment is mostly according to themes but there is some step-by-step exegesis, notably of the Cana miracle, the multiplication of the loaves, and the raising of Lazarus. The positions taken might be called historically conservative.

John Painter's *Reading John's Gospel Today* (Atlanta, 1980), 158 pages, is a slighter effort. It appeared formerly as *John, Witness and Theologian* (London, 1975), 160 pages. After an introduction he devotes part 2 to the Gospel's theology and part 3 to interpreting 1 Jn, with a concluding part 4 on "John's Symbolism: Word Symbol or Sacrament?" in which he holds that symbolism is so broad in Jn that the rites of baptism and Eucharist have no exclusive function there. "The evangelist is no sacramentalist in this [viz., Bultmann's] sense" (p. 139). That he might be a sacramentalist in a late-first-century sense is not taken into account.

Robert Kysar has produced three extremely helpful studies over a decade. The first is *John, the Maverick Gospel* (Atlanta, 1976), 119 pages, reckoned by Robin Scroggs to be the best non-technical introduction to the FG. Based on the landmark commentaries available at the time in English, it is distinguished by its excellence as a pedagogical tool. Another simpler work but equally enlightening is *John's Story of Jesus* (Philadelphia, 1984),

96 pages. A diagram on the spiraling character of the Nicodemus discourse is illustrative of the construction of all the discourses. A schematic overview of the signs and speeches of chapters 2 through 5 is another helpful device. The observation that "Jesus' life and ministry are the re-creation of the Jewish faith" (p. 24) is closer to the mark than an earlier observation, "Torah is indeed the revelation of God, but Jesus is the further revelation which supersedes the Law" (p. 18). Two themes are isolated as paramount in Jn's concern: Jesus' transforming and fulfilling of Hebraic tradition, and the role of the witnesses to Christ's truth. Kysar's division of the Gospel is interesting: Beginnings (1:1–51); Jesus Reveals Glory (2:1–12:50); Jesus Receives Glory (13:1–20:29); and Endings (20:30–21:25). Perhaps the most ambitious, although not the most ingenious, of his three books is *John,* in the Augsburg Commentary on the New Testament (Minneapolis, 1986), 331 pages. This book "for lay people, students and pastors" is written in running prose and says something about every verse. It has no foreign words or phrases and no footnotes but is remarkably comprehensive.

Brown had produced an "updating summary" of his researches on Jn a decade after the appearance of the second volume on the Gospel and in anticipation of the book on the epistles then in preparation. This exploration of the development of the Johannine church is entitled *The Community of the Beloved Disciple* (New York/Mahwah, 1979), 204 pages. It stemmed from Brown's presidential address to the Society of Biblical Literature and his Shaffer Lectures at the Yale Divinity School. He traces hypothetically the progress of a group of Jewish believers in Jesus from a relatively "low" Christology (Messiah, prophet, servant, Lord, Son of God, in the sense of divine representative) to a "high" one (Jesus within the sphere of divinity, Lord and Son of God in a more exalted sense, and even the designation "God"). The leader in this transition was a disciple who would come to be known as "the disciple whom Jesus loved." It was catalyzed by the adherence to the movement of Jews of anti-Temple bias who made converts in

Samaria and brought on debates with other Jews who thought the movement constituted an abandonment of strict monotheism. Gentile Greeks of the Diaspora joined the community. These developments, coupled with the commitment to a high Christology against Jews and Jewish Christians of a more traditional faith persuasion, led to a third phase, a split within the community. The adherents of the author of the epistles (the "presbyter") witnessed the departure of the secessionists, calling them children of the devil and antichrists. Their offense was affirming that *knowledge* of God's Son was all-important and denying the full humanity of one who was divine, as he was. Those in the presbyter's party who confessed that Jesus had come in the flesh held that anointing with the Spirit obviated the need for human teachers. They went on to accept presbyter-bishops as authoritative teachers in the second century. This group was gradually assimilated into the great church, while the larger number of the Johannine community seem to have moved to Gnosticism of a docetic variety.

D. Moody Smith's *John,* in Fortress's Proclamation Series (second rev. ed.; Philadelphia, 1986), 133 pages, is not a verse commentary so much as a treatment of themes, but with exegesis of the prologue (1:1–18), chs. 5, 9, 16, and 1 Jn. An introductory part 1 discusses the FG's characteristics and structure, distinguishing between Jesus' public ministry and his ministry to his disciples. After the exegetical portion illustrative of the Johannine perspective past and present comes the final part 3, Interpretation. There, a number of aspects are discussed: historical origins of the Gospel, theological factors influencing the development of Jn's thought, and the task of interpreting an interpretation, which the FG is. The revised edition adds to the earliest part discussions of the relation of Jn to the Synoptics and also to the epistles, and to the third part an extensive literary analysis.

Bruce E. Schein takes the reader on a walking tour of the places named in Jn's Gospel. This tireless Lutheran topographer has tramped every mile more than once and reports it in his *Following the Way: The Setting of John's Gospel* (Minneapolis,

1980), 223 pages. He may discourage some—and encourage others—by his seeming acceptance of the Fourth Gospel as a day-book of Jesus' journeys, but that noncritical view of history does nothing to cloud his critical faculties when it comes to geography and archaeology. This is a most informative book.

Daniel Harrington, SJ, writes in his customary workman-like fashion of the structure, purpose, and key ideas of the FG in *John's Thought and Theology: An Introduction* (Wilmington, 1990), 120 pages, while **William S. Kurz, SJ,** examines Jn 13–17 among *The Farewell Addresses in the New Testament* (Wilmington, 1990).

Josef Blank, in *The Gospel according to St. John,* gen. ed. John L. McKenzie, 3 vols. (New York, 1981), derives his researches in Johannine Christology and eschatology from his scholarly *Krisis* of 1964. The German series in which the shorter books appear is directed toward Christian prayer. Blank's volumes regularly divide pericopes into "exegesis" and "meditation" but the author is obviously ill at ease in the second part. This results in a useful but dull summary of exegetical findings throughout.

The largest success in this category comes from a Dutch Mill Hill Missionary based in England, **John Wijngaards.** His *The Gospel of John and His Letters,* ed. Carolyn Osiek, is volume 11 in the Message of Biblical Spirituality Series (Wilmington, 1986), 304 pages. The three sections of the book, in the thirty brief chapters, are entitled Turning towards the Light, The Father, and Abundance of Life. The subheadings of the last section are: Inherited Autonomy, Involvement and Service, and Liberating Dreams. The text is replete with poetic and other literary references while the notes reflect acquaintance with a broad body of scholarship. The Gospel is divided into "seven weeks—seven signs." This and other pedagogical devices may startle the fastidious but, all things considered, the book is an ingenious incentive to reflection and prayer.

James McCaffrey's doctoral dissertation from the Pontifical Biblical Institute on two verses of Jn takes the position that they are deliberately open to two readings: that the faith in him demanded by Jesus (14:1b), acknowledging the apprehension experienced by the disciples at his impending departure in death (see 13:37 f.), gives them the pledge of his ongoing presence (cf. 14:23) but also promises reunion with them at the end time in the heavenly house of his Father (vv. 2–3).[83]

Finally, **Gerard Sloyan**'s *John* (Atlanta, 1988), 276 pages, regularly attempts to go beyond the exegetical, with what success it is for the reader to say. On balance it must be maintained that no one has yet come up to the combination of scholarship and piety achieved by Sir Edwyn Hoskyns in his commentary of 1940.

4
Treatments of Johannine Themes

Anyone who chooses for scrutiny one aspect or a cluster of related themes in the FG runs the risk of being charged with neglect of equally important themes. But since no one can discuss anything under all aspects at the same time, the writer who isolates a Johannine concern is not to be faulted. Attention to any segment of John's thought brings in its train so much besides that exploring even a brief pericope poses for the author the problem of where to stop. Most solve the problem by citing a wide range of literature that falls outside their immediate field, as a way of both directing readers further and assuring their peers that they are aware of all the opinions they did not incorporate. This final chapter needs to consider the treatments of several individual themes or problems in the FG. Invariably, if the works are of book length, they will touch on many other questions.

Mark Stibbe anthologizes in *The Gospel of John as Literature* essays on the literary form and theology of the FG, the earliest being that on irony by G. MacRae (1973).[1] John D. Crossan contributes a structuralist analysis of John 6 while Werner Kelber discovers in "The Birth of a Beginning: John 1:1–18" three beginnings, one of the preexistent Logos (vv. 1–5), another of John and his witness (vv. 6–18, 15), and a third, Jesus' earthly beginning (v. 14). Stibbe's "John's Gospel" employs the by-now familiar technique of reader-response criticism, heading his chapters Hero, Plot, Genre, Style, and Polemic. Jesus is called an elusive hero described by an elusive author who provides only nineteen frugal "asides" to suggest his thoughts, motives, and attitudes. Over 55 percent of the FG's verbs are taken up with his deeds or words, from which the author's characterization of him must be deduced. Stibbe uses A. J. Greimas's universal structure of narrative possibilities (*Semantique structurale,* 1966) to show that the plot of the Gospel contains a true plot, namely, of the devil against Jesus' life. As to the literary genre, the passion account is a tragedy set within a biography, but the FG overall has the U-shaped plot of the mythos of comedy. It ends with a springtime of Jesus' being lifted up to depart and ascend to glory. The comedic elements thus come at the beginning, a wedding feast, and at the end, a meal of joyous reunion at the lakeshore, with the Risen One supplying a surfeit of food.

John Ashton's anthology *The Interpretation of John* updates the first edition of 1986 and appears in a series that collects and reproduces key studies previously published.[2] The fifteen selections range in date from Rudolph Bultmann's article on Jesus as the emissary of God in the prologue (1923) to Martin C. DeBoer's piece on the narrative and historical criticism directed to John's Gospel. The contributors whose book-length work is not reported on in the pages to follow are Paul Lamarche (1964), Ignace de la Potterie (1977), Peder Borgen (1968), Günther Bornkamm (1968), Nils A. Dahl (1962), J.-A. Bühner (1977), and Stephen D. Moore (1993). Lamarche writing on the prologue maintains that the vocabulary is that of a Greek-speaking Semite but that the words in verses 1–9 convey God's interest through the Logos in the Gentile world and 10–11 in Israel; 14–18 are again devoted to Israel and parallel the concern of 1–9 for the Gentiles. It is evident from 12–13 despite certain rebuffs, 10–11, that God from the beginning planned to unite the two in a single community. Lamarche sees in the much-argued "bloods" of verse 13 the two ethnic stocks, neither able to claim dominance. If "his own"

(v. 11) means Jesus' people Israel, then the nearby "world" of verse 10 is the Gentile world, accounting for a double rejection of the Logos. *Tà ídia,* a neuter plural, could mean both home and Temple; but the people itself is that home of God. As to similarities in the writings of the apostolic age, Lamarche sees a greater likeness of the prologue to Ephesians 1:1–4, especially the "we" and "you" of verses 12 and 13, than to the usual candidate, the Christ hymn of Colossians 1:15–20.

Bühner goes against the popular wisdom by maintaining that the center of gravity in an "I am" saying is not Jesus but the predicate nominative, usually accompanied by a judicial statement that applies it to the salvation of believers. Hence, "I am" is not necessarily a revelation formula but the self-identification of a messenger. The basic element of the message is a promise. Jesus is bread, door, shepherd, vine, light, way, truth, and life as pictorial concretizations of the functional message/messenger relationship. God has appointed him alone as mediator between God and the human race. "Through the proclamation of God's sending his emissary, Jesus' word becomes the life-bestowing and life-giving word of God, and the whole significance of this word is concentrated in the person of the emissary."[3] Stephen D. Moore imagines the story of the woman of Samaria to mean not only her thirst but Jesus' desire to slake it with living water and his Father's desire to have true worshippers. Tracking the living waters that flow out of Jesus' heart (lit., belly) or the believer's (7:38), his thirst on the cross "in order to fulfill the scripture" (19:28), and the water flowing from Jesus' side (v. 34), Moore concludes that the water imagery in John is a river of desire, a desire of Jesus to return to his Father and, at the time of the Gospel's composition, a stream that flows to earth, the Paraclete. Ashton distances himself from this kind of literary interpretation but includes it as representative of much contemporary writing and, although he does not say it, patristic as well. Günther Bornkamm (1968) takes on Käsemann's *Testament of Jesus,* calling it helpful in promoting awareness of the paradoxes and puzzles of the FG but too one-sided to give an accurate account of the Gospel's peculiar dialectic.

A collection of papers honoring D. Moody Smith on his sixty-fifth birthday provides a means to come abreast of some of the best of contemporary Johannine scholarship. *Exploring the Gospel of John* (**R. A. Culpepper** and **C. C. Black,** eds.) includes contributions of the following authors besides those whose recent work will be commented on below: Davies, Borgen, Barrett, Beutler, Dunn, Gaventa, Keck, Martyn, Meeks, P. Meyer, Schweizer, Segovia, Smalley, and Weder.[4] All of the essays are historical and hermeneutical; none has a pastoral component except by indirection. Some writers repeat positions from previous book-length work, for example, Davies' continued acceptance of the now widely repudiated theory of the public recitation of the Twelfth Benediction of eighteen (*Shemone Esre,* actually nineteen and this one a curse), first proposed by M. von Aberle in 1861 as a way to catch out Jesus-believing Jews. A number of papers explore a particular theme or treatment in the FG; thus: parables (Schweizer), rhetoric (Black), God (Meyer), pneumatology (Smalley), and ethics (Meeks), while Dunn explores the difference between John and the Synoptics as a theological problem. Charlesworth summarizes much of the three books he has authored or co-authored on the Dead Sea Scrolls, including one on John in relation to them (1991). He concludes that, while no connection with the Jesus movement can be established, the Qumrân and John communities possessed a common view of the religion of Israel and its vocabulary of the time, even though the Righteous Teacher and Jesus interpreted it differently and the post-Yavneh Hillelites in still a third way. One vocabulary example is the scrolls' *derek* and the gospels' *hodos,* both seemingly having preceded the Rabbis' *halakah,* for "way."

Peder Borgen identifies in John 3:13 a polemic against visionaries who claim a heavenly ascent within a Jewish context. Unlike many, he sees mention of the Samaritans and the Greeks as indications that the Johannine community has moved beyond ethnic Jewish boundaries, and seems to take the undoubted cosmic dimension of the FG as a "movement toward internationalization," although he states the proposition in reverse. Fernando Segovia modestly retracts a former view with his acknowledgment that the perceived aporias in the text are not attributable to a process of accretion and redaction but can be explained in simpler ways. On balance he now thinks the Gospel a fairly unitary and consistent product, even while the apparently "disruptive aporias" in chapters 15–16 remain. Leander Keck provides an ingenious exploration of what is of God and what is man in Jesus by exegeting the main passages that contain the preposition *èk,* including for completeness' sake what is of or from flesh or the devil. He finds "of-ness" to be the key to the Gospel's Christology but also "part of Jesus' distinctive revelatory proclamation." **Beverly Roberts Gaventa**'s brief paper tackles the problem of the dual endings of chapters 20 and 21 and says that the solution lies in an "archive of excess." The author of the first twenty chapters solved the problem of bringing his narrative to a close by having Jesus return to the Father, leaving behind a stable group of followers. The other author thought a different kind of closure necessary (an anti-closure?). And so he opened up the futures of Peter and the beloved disciple, knowing that "Jesus' story will never close." The 153 fish, the net that did not break, and the breakfast ready on the shore before the seine is hauled in are all signs of an excess that is only beginning to express itself. Lastly the co-editor, **C. Clifton Black,** first culls passages from ancient writers who thought grand stylization to be appropriate for matters pertaining to divinity. He then goes on to analyze the circular redundancy of clauses and topics in John, providing "amplification" as the technical term for this vertiginous style. Classical rhetoric is cited for examples of refining or polishing, the punning repetition of a word in two senses, enumerating the parts of a whole, and synonymy. All these provide the "hypnotic range of repetitive figures" used by John (see 14:27; 17:18; 14:1, 2b–3, 7 for examples). This stylistic affinity with modes of Graeco-Roman discourse is hardly a retraction of Semitic influence on John. Black concludes that by his careful scrutiny of Jesus' leave-taking in 14–17 and the way deity and humanity converge in him in the Gospel, he has identified the basis for the same convergence in the community of 1 John. Black is convinced he has effectively challenged the long-standing appraisal of Blass-Debrunner's *Greek Grammar* (260): "The absence of rhetorical art in the Johannine discourses is quite clear." For him it is its presence that is clear.

Coming abreast of the material in the above three collections would be one way of discovering where the Johannine scholarship in English or English translation stands in the twenty-first century. Other readers need assurance of its results in more popular expository form. For this a number of satisfactory titles have been produced, among them **R. Alan Culpepper**'s *The Gospel and Letters of John*[5] and **D. Moody Smith**'s *The Theology of the Gospel of John*.[6] Culpepper draws on his more than twenty years of John scholarship to proceed methodically from an opening chapter that introduces the Johannine writings to three successive chapters on the Gospel (1–4; 5–12; 13–21), then one on the letters and a concluding treatment of "The Gospel as a Document of Faith." The book is admirably designed for pedagogic purposes and might well serve as a college or adult education text, or even as an orientation to semester-length study in a seminary or graduate course. Smith has written a helpful programmatic survey in a series devoted to the theology of the individual NT writings that gives him a chance to summarize his academic lifetime of Jn studies. Hellenism, Gnosticism, and the Dead Sea Scrolls first receive an exposition, then a survey of the Gospel's content, chapter by chapter. The book concludes with remarks on its relation to the three epistles and to Revelation, to Pauline Christianity and Hebrews, plus the Nag Hammadi Gospel of Truth and the Odes of Solomon. Surprisingly, Smith's attempt to express delicately what emerged as Christianity is less than sure-footed: "The Gospel of John seems to be thoroughly supersessionist...for it anticipates the displacement of Jews as

God's people by Christians and appropriates the Jewish scripture as its own (5:39, 45–47)," followed immediately by "We have no king but Caesar" (19:15) as if that shout, authored by Jn, expressed "a disavowing of the lordship of God"[7] in that or any century. What we see taking place in Jn is not "the self-definition" of both sides, Judaism's becoming what it is "by virtue of the rejection of this claim [that Jesus was the Messiah of Israel]."[8] The claim is clearly made in the FG and just as clearly reported on as rejected by others in the locale of the Gospel's composition, but Judaism became what it is through many affirmations, not one denial, and Christianity the same. Professor Smith cites **Alan Segal**'s *Rebecca's Children* (1986) helpfully in pondering the question,[9] where Segal correctly has Judaism or Rabbinism and Christianity each coming to slow birth from the womb of the religion of Israel, rather than the church from the synagogue as in the reading of Jn that Christianity adopted. There are many riches in a short compass in this treatment of John's theology. Wrestling with the problem of which Jews Jn intended as resisters to his message (his contemporaries must have very well known) would not have removed a problem of the ages but would have made this valuable book a stronger offering.

For more popular treatments than the above two but equally useful, there are **Raymond F. Collins**'s *John and His Witness*,[10] **Stanley B. Marrow**'s *The Gospel of John: A Reading*,[11] **Andreas J. Köstenberger**'s *Encountering John: The Gospel in Historical, Literary, and Theological Perspective*,[12] and **Robert Kysar**'s *Preaching John*.[13] Collins's work is sketched in swift strokes of 112 pages and derives from his heavier *These Things Have Been Written* of one year before.[14] The John of the title is the Baptist, a designation the FG does not use. His witness to Jesus is the title of the first chapter and after that The First Disciples, Andrew, Simon Peter, Philip, and Nathanael, and an epilogue. The text reads smoothly while the footnote citations are to the first-rate European and American scholarship one expects from a then-professor of the University of Louvain (since at the Catholic University of America with F. J. Moloney). Marrow, an Iraq-born New England province Jesuit, writes at length in *The Gospel of John: A Reading* but without the apparatus of the academy to which he belongs. His is, as the subtitle says, a reading to which he invites the reader to accompany him. His technique is to print intermittently in bold-face one or several verses representative of longer passages and follow them with his reflections. These are directed to individuals rather than to the wider community of believers. Marrow has the advantage of command of a living Semitic tongue as do few contemporary Western interpreters of John. He cites A. M. Rihbany, author of *The Syrian Christ* (1920), as another. There are, of course, translations of the Bible in Arabic and, for those who know biblical Hebrew, the United Bible Society's New Testament in modern Hebrew, which renders John 1:1 "and God was the Word," which is faithful to the Greek word order.[15] Andreas Köstenberger has been given by his publisher a handsome pictographic and pedagogic treatment of his verse commentary, with an even wider range of photographs than Bruce Schein's *Following in the Way*. A previous note states that "since John is at the core a *religious* book with a *spiritual* message, and since Christianity is at the core a *historical* religion," it cannot be studied on merely historical or literary terms. Köstenberger favors a prima facie approach to John's twenty-one chapters, namely, that everything happened just as recorded. At the same time, he relies on and cites in endnotes the best of critical scholarship. The paradox is sustained throughout. There is no indication that chapter 21 might be the word of another hand, the epistles are taken to be the work of the evangelist, and "the Jewish nation at large, represented by its religious leadership, had rejected the God-sent Messiah." That position is maintained in a detailed excursus which concludes that, although the Jews of Jesus' day "had become part of the unbelieving world," John's Gospel is not anti-Semitic.

Robert Kysar had produced three titles on the FG and one on the epistles before publishing *Preaching John*. Many readers other than homilists can profit from this work, which presents first the questions of authorship, mode of composition, and overriding theme in simple language from a critical viewpoint. Kysar is committed to the theory that the evangelist, followed by his final editor, intentionally wrote at two levels, primarily that of their situation in the late first century, using words and deeds of Jesus from the remembered tradition as their raw material. The book is helpful in warning against certain traps like interpreting John in the spirit of some other New Testament author or authors, reading his symbolism literally, or castigating "the Jews" without troubling to discover who might be meant by this baffling phrase. Aside from supposing that they are somehow "the religious establishment" he does not delve more deeply into the problem. Like the work of Culpepper and Smith above, this small volume could serve admirably to introduce a reader to "what they are saying about John" with the added benefit of suggesting what not to say about this literary corpus. He also provides a number of sample sermons based on John readings in *The Revised Common Lectionary* (1992).

At this point it may be well to name some important full-scale commentaries on the FG and epistles of John that have appeared in the last decade. Two multivolume works take a position on almost every passage and verse in the Gospel, that of an Australian Salesian of Don Bosco[16] and a French member of the Society of Jesus,[17] while two single-volume commentaries are the work of a member of a Methodist faculty of divinity[18] and a Baptist professor who has been president of the Catholic Biblical Association of America.[19] Looking at the four in sequence, we find that of **Francis Moloney** and **Xavier Léon-Dufour** to be similar to Kysar's in that both are alerted to the way this Gospel is read, heard, and preached in the church. Moloney favors a reader-response approach that he combines with the critical. The leisurely three and four volumes respectively have a little more "sap" than is usual in historical exegesis. That is certainly true of **Gail O'Day**'s comments, whose extensive work on John follows the pattern of the multivolume commentary in which it appears. A lengthy introduction to the Gospel comes first, then an exegetical commentary of high quality with the NRSV translation on facing pages, and in third place "Reflections." Here the scholar acts as teacher by applying the text to modern life in a most intelligent manner. **Charles Talbert** wears his scholarship lightly in a deceptively simple commentary, first on the three letters and then on the Gospel. He assumes along with Segovia (1982) and Grayston (1984) that the letters were written either before the Gospel or at the same time (Strecker, 1989) and in the order 2, 3, 1, as in Marshall (1978), the FG's final form having come "either alongside or after 1 John" (4). Refreshingly, there are no foot- or endnotes; all the references including those to rabbinic material are incorporated into the text. Regrettably, no indexes are provided.

The Dutch exegete **Herman Ridderbos** had his theological commentary of 587 pages translated into English in 1997 and theological it undoubtedly is, for it finds the church's later faith positions on many pages of the Gospel.[20] Previous to that, an Irish Dominican, **Thomas Brodie,** published two distinct volumes in 1993, one a quest for the FG's sources and the other a full-blown commentary.[21] In the first of these he opts for a transformative process of written sources like that of Virgil retelling Homer, the Bible, and the *midrashim*. He rejects a generalized orality as a source, dependence on the Synoptics, especially a finally edited Mark, and theories of successive editings of John by the original author or another hand. His argument seems more convincing in a general way than in its many particulars. The one we call John, in sum, framed a series of coherent narratives and reflections derived from many places in already existing writings. Brodie's commentary is literary and theological as the subtitle says, precisely not historical or social-historical. The canonical version is the one the author intended except for the later-added 7:53–8:11. Aporias and contradictions are literary devices either to catch the reader up short or to show development in Jesus' thought as the author presents it. All that the Gospel recounts is taken as having happened to Jesus, although the commentator is fully aware that he is dealing with an artfully woven narrative calculated to persuade the hearer that a new *life* in the Spirit Paraclete is available in the risen and ascended Jesus. Francis Moloney wrote his *The Gospel according to John* after his three-book commentary and does not hesitate to draw on it but goes deeper into problems of interpretation and cites the solutions of many scholars.[22] It is the perfect exemplar of the *genus* one-volume commentary in a series. If the book has a flaw, it is one that it shares with all of its type: The verse the reader wishes the author to take a position on is passed over in silence. Some diligent researcher should make an anthology of such missed opportunities in all the major commentaries! A major effort is **Seán P. Kealy**'s two-volume work, each of some 500 pages, in which he evaluates hundreds of works interpreting Jn from the earliest centuries until now.[23] It is unique in cataloguing works on Jn by century, book 1 from the second to the nineteenth centuries, book 2 exclusively of the twentieth. Latin, German, and English titles, a few in French, are critiqued by the author, excerpted from, and portions of reviews given. We shall not soon again see the like of this rich plum cake of a scholarly work.

Kenneth Grayston's commentary on the FG published late in the twentieth century is righty termed "deceptively simple." It has several virtues, starting with its brevity, but one in particular is the author's gift for rendering puzzling phrases in modern English, for example, 8:25; 13:10; and especially, "Do not let your resolution be upset" at 14:1, 27.[24] **Donald A Carson** of Illinois' Trinity Divinity School followed him shortly with his 715-page *The Gospel according to John,* which holds it to be an evangelistic gospel. The adjective proves not redundant when the author's meaning comes clear.[25] Aware of the evangelist's familiarity with the Jewish scriptures and pilgrimage feasts and supposing that the Johannine Christians already knew the content of the Gospel, Carson assumes that it had to be written not "*to* believers *about* mission but *to* outsiders to *perform* mission."[26] In other words, "diaspora Jews and proselytes to Judaism constitute the only possibility." This is but one of many points on which he thinks the major contemporary commentators have it wrong, spelling out his argument each time. Quoting Barrett, Brown, Dodd,

Beasley-Murray, and Schnackenburg frequently but not always in agreement, he acquaints readers with the opinions of writers on John whose work readers of the present summary may not readily come upon.

Twenty-four European and North American scholars exchanged papers as a result of a four-year University of Leuven research program on the alleged anti-Judaism of the Gospel of John.[27] The positions taken are so rich and many that only an examination of the volume will do it justice. Eleven of the twenty-four contributors—Catholics, Protestants, and one Jew— are book authors cited elsewhere in these pages. The editors provide an introductory "Analysis of the Current Debate" indicating what to look for in the various essays. Some of the extremely diverse conclusions are as follows: The period 70–135 was marked by disparate religious positions taken by Jews on the religion of Israel (uncommonly "Judaism") to interpret the meaning of the destruction of the city and Temple; the early developed positions of the infant church (incarnation, triune name of God, full religious equality of Jews and Gentiles) necessarily distanced it from the bulk of Jewish people; no attempts to reconstruct the tensions between the Jesus Jews and the Moses/Temple Jews (add in Samaritans and Qumranites) can diminish the ill effect of the FG as it stands on centuries of bad Christian relations with Jews. Of the many papers that wrestle with who exactly the hostile *Ioudaîoi* were, only two hint obliquely that a certain elite might have thought themselves the Jews *kat'exochēn,* but none says clearly that it was a self-designation that the evangelist was familiar with but did not invent.

Turning to recent literature on the epistles, mention should first be made of the magisterial work of **Rudolph Schnackenburg,** whose 7th edition (1984) was Englished by Reginald and Ilse Fuller eight years later.[28] **Georg Strecker**'s commentary of 1989 received similar treatment in a translation of Linda Maloney in 1996.[29] At a somewhat simpler but scholarly level are the works of **David Rensberger** referred to above (ch. 3, nn. 25–32)[30] and

Colin G. Kruse.[31] More modest still but thoroughly dependable is the running commentary of the Australian **William Loader,**[32] roughly at the level of **Gerard S. Sloyan**'s,[33] on limitations set by the respective series' editors. Far more detailed than the four immediately above and including the text in Greek is **Judith Lieu**'s exploration of 2 and 3 John based on the author's University of Birmingham doctoral dissertation.[34] This is a technical exposition of the mutual relation of the two epistles to 1 John and of that treatise in turn to the Gospel. Her shorter work titled *The Theology of the Johannine Epistles* is largely confined to a discussion of 1 John.[35] It traces the epistle's theology through a number of themes: knowing him (whether God or Jesus is not always clear); being born of God as God's children; abiding in and having love of God and love in the community.

Attending now to writings of the last decade on the FG, first in order is the collection of thirty-eight papers on the text of John in relation to the Synoptics delivered at the Thirty-Ninth Biblical Colloquium at Leuven, Belgium, in 1990 and dedicated to retiring Professor **Frans Neirynck.**[36] The papers are largely in French or English with a few in German and respond in one way or another to Neirynck's long-held position that the FG had the first three as its sources, reversing what had become a consensus since the days of Windisch (1926) and Gardner-Smith (1938). **D. Moody Smith**'s little book on the same question reports the opinions of several major twentieth-century exegetes and ends with the word that ambiguity remains (185).[37] A special benefit of his book is the clarity with which he lays out **Boismard**'s complex theory of dependence (with **Lamouille**),[38] in which he is aided by Neirynck's chart of the theory that is as much needed as a key to *Finnegan's Wake*. Smith gives a critical response to Boismard that one can agree with by wielding Ockham's razor as he does and arriving at a dependence theory of remarkable simplicity (139–58). Any who have wrestled with the problem will cherish Smith's remarkable gift of grasp and clear prose.

The studies of the FG that appeared in English in the 1990s are so varied in theme and treatment that any attempt to categorize them might end in failure. For that reason the date of the appearance of each from earliest to latest seems a practical solution. The cascade of published titles means that those listed or commented on below are necessarily a fraction. A report on what may be the most insightful book of the decade is left to the end.

Seven members of the Society for the Study of the New Testament delivered papers on the Shepherd Discourse of John 10, which **Johannes Beutler, SJ,** and **Robert Fortna** edited.[39] **Ulrich Busse** finds a functional unity of Jesus with God in 10:24–38 (despite v. 33), rather than the unity of substance that the christological councils saw in v. 30. **John Painter** discovers in the evangelist's Christology "a functional and an ontological sonship, an emissary and incarnational christology." The *paroimía* of 10:1–5 has Jesus the shepherd in conflict with thieves and robbers, strangers whose voice the sheep do not recognize, but at a secondary level the shepherd is the evangelist as leader or leaders of the Jn community. In this early segment the Baptist is the gatekeeper who will be more clearly identified as the door to salvation in 7–10. Jesus is the good shepherd of 11–18 but now one who lays down his life and takes it up again, a development for which verses 1–5 have not prepared the hearer. The hireling and the wolf have not appeared in the earlier figure, but now, rather than representing the leaders of the people who do not believe in Jesus, they are the embattled false teachers within the community itself. Jesus is not identical with God, "who is greater than all" (v. 29). He is, however, one with the Father in doing the work and will of the Father (v. 30; cf. 5:18). "Son of God," a title ascribed to Jesus in 10:36 and by implication in vv. 15, 17, 18, "is justified in that Jesus is demonstrably the emissary of God. The works are the evidence." **M. Sabbe** of the Leuven school not surprisingly finds similarities in this segment with the Synoptics, notably the dispersal of the sheep (v. 12) with Mk's use of Zech 13:7 in 14:27 (cf. Mt 26:31) and the shepherd's willingness to lay down his life (v. 11) as close to Mk 10:45. The latter immediately precedes, as does Jn 10, what Sabbe calls "an anticipated Passion Narrative." **J. A. du Rand** is complex, calling on the Greimasian square and C. Bremond's narratological model (both with charts), and S. Rimmon-Kenan's identification of a narrative as a story event both "after later events have been told and before earlier events have been mentioned." The writer shows how the plot and point of view of the author-narrator elicit both sympathy and antipathy toward the various characters, Jesus included.

Donald Senior, CP, in the fourth of his brief books on each gospel's passion narrative provides in a preface and first chapter a summary of the kind of writing the FG is, its major themes, and who Jesus is for those who already believe in him.[40] The book then examines the following pericopes exegetically after important flashbacks to chapters 7, 10, 11, and 14–17: (1) 18:1–11; (2) 18:12–27; (3) 18:28—19:16; and (4) 19:17–42. One cannot imagine a better commentary in this brief a compass than the one the Chicago Theological Union Passionist has provided. The foot washing of John 13 is explored by **John Christopher Thomas,** who is a professor at the Church of God School of Theology in Cleveland, Tennessee.[41] G. Richter and W. Lohse had both done the same in their dissertations of 1967. Thomas concludes first that vv. 6–10 and 12–20 constitute a unity and cannot be played off against one another, then that Peter's initial demurrer is a case of Johannine misunderstanding that Jesus must explain, not the confusion of an inferior at an offer of hospitality by a superior. Thomas's more important deduction is that, as foot washing in Jewish and Graeco-Roman antiquity was normally done to prepare for something, its occurrence in the FG suggests an introduction to the entire Last Supper discourse. It conveys a cleansing that supplements the bath (baptism) that has earlier produced a more fundamental cleansing (3:5–7). He further speculates that the Jn community had foot washing as a religious rite as part of its preoccupation with postconversion sin, as evidenced in 1 John. A last chapter reflects on whether the ritual had a sacramental character for the community and why the Synoptics do not mention it. It contains summaries and quotations of writings of the church fathers on the practice to the year 400. Some speak of it in conjunction with the forgiveness of sins. Thomas wonders if Jn features it because they were already experiencing violent persecution. ("No slave is greater than his master nor any messenger greater than the one who sent him," v. 16).

Fernando F. Segovia's many individual articles culminate in *The Farewell of the Word* (1991), an exhaustive study of the discourses beginning at 19:31 and leading up to chapter 17.[42] He hopes to provide a reading that "brings the artistic and strategic dimensions of the farewell closely together, from both a synchronic and diachronic perspective."[43] The following units of discourse are examined at chapter length: 13:31—14:31; 15:1–17; 15:18—16:4a; 16:4b–33. A structural outline of each comes first, then a tracking of its literary organization and development, ending with a synchronic proposal that features the discourse's strategic flow. At all points there is revealed a working out of the beginning announcement of Jesus' glorification in 13:31–32. The language of the analysis is technical, not literary. **A. T. Hanson** updates two previous books of 1965 and 1980, quoting from them copiously in his search for a word, a phrase, or a sentence from scripture, in what he calls *The Prophetic Gospel*.[44] Successive chapters examine the FG from the prologue to the risen life accounts, noting which scholars do or do not hold specific passages to betray either an awareness of or an intent to employ particular biblical passages. "The whole book is founded in scripture"[45] and "we cannot fail to be impressed by the variety and depth of Jn's spiritual store."[46] Hanson maintains that he can distinguish between texts "received from tradition and those which he discovered for himself,"[47] citing passages from 18–19 as examples. Citations from the FG in Greek are translated but then a variety of possibilities underlying them follows in other languages: Hebrew text, LXX, Aramaic targums, Qumrân, Vulgate. "John was well acquainted with Jewish methods of exegesis of scripture...he must have had access to Aramaic literature and tradition also...[and]

must have known something of Paul's theology."[48] The philological exploration is exhaustive and includes the unusual opinion that the LXX is a translation of the MT rather than of some other text. Hanson proposes the probable theological use made of each scriptural text the evangelist employs. His overall conclusion is that this is a theological rather than a historical writing. The worth of the study lies in the identification of the many dozens of Old Testament echoes found in Jn. **Margaret Davies** deals with the FG as the narrative that it is in *Rhetoric and Reference in the Fourth Gospel,* where her attention to the usual considerations (omniscient narrator, story time, plot, characters, implied author, implied reader) is regularly obscured by her attention to the smallest details along the way.[49] At an early point she expresses dissatisfaction with writers who see the Gospel as docetic (Käsemann) or subordinationist (Haenchen) and hopes to demonstrate the cause of the confusion, namely, their taking John's "Son of God" to mean the eternal Son synonymous with *logos* rather than Jesus as a Jew who is the Jewish Messiah. The assumption that *doxa* means the glory of divinity rather than the honor or respect due the human Jesus is held to be part of the confusion. The "Reference" of the title is unclear but may mean that in Jn reference refers to the world, the "Jews," eschatology, Palestinian geography, and cultural history. Davies thinks the Gospel's portrayal of the Jews, if meant for the time of its composition, to be a "gross caricature" since in that period the Sh‘ma was being recited twice daily with its commandments to love God and fellow humans. In brief, the trees of multiple verbal exegesis make it hard to see the woods of the story. *The Word in the World* of Canadian scholar **Adele Reinhartz** had its origins in a dissertation that began as a history of religions study of John 10:1–5.[50] It ends with the conclusion that "for the Fourth Evangelist, Jesus is the divinely sent King whose jurisdiction and power extend over the world of both the living and the dead."[51] Reinhartz employs the vocabulary of reader-response criticism to analyze the cosmological tale (she calls it a meta-tale) that dominates the narrative's historical and ecclesiological tales. Jesus' coming down from above upon a world of darkness and sin is the burden of the *paroimía* of the shepherd whose sheep know his voice, in a cosmological reading of the text. The shepherd is the Word, the sheep are humankind, the sheepfold is the world, the thief or robber Satan, and the gatekeeper John the Baptist. This reading requires seeing the shepherd's entry into the fold as a descent, for Reinhartz a figure of Jesus' domination of the cosmos to which he has brought life and light. His "own sheep" are believers whom he is dedicated to protect.[52] The censures of bad shepherds in Ezekiel 34 and Zechariah 11 plus the motif of Jesus' kingship in 1:49; 6:15; 12:13, 15; 13:33–37; 18:36–37, in which the ruler of this world is condemned (16:11) and his realm overcome (16:33), are her warrant. The similitude is between a simple pastoral scene and a timeless cosmic struggle.

Jeffrey Trumbower essays an anthropology of the FG in *Born from Above,* in which he tackles a problem that goes back to Origen's refutation of the Gnostic Heracleon.[53] He accused the Valentinians of holding that the Samaritan woman was of the *pneumatic* type, hence destined to be saved, the royal official of Jn 4 a *psychic* or one able to choose, and some unbelievers in Jesus of chapter 8 *hylics* (materialists) incapable of salvation. Trumbower's problem is hence one of long standing: whether Jn gives evidence of containing a pre-Gnostic strain in which believers in Jesus possess an affinity to a higher realm of knowledge or truth that constitutes an absolute rather than a conditioned predestination to salvation. His first, tentative conclusion is that an earlier version of the prologue and other passages were so disposed but were modified by a later editorial hand. Augustine, Luther, and Calvin read Jn 8 especially through a Pauline lens. They concluded that a radical change from slavery to sin to slavery to God is possible by God's grace. Adolf Hilgenfeld alone in a commentary on the Gospel and epistles (1849) stood with Heracleon in writing that the Gospel "is a systematic gnostic treatise, complete with a Marcionite demiurge, John 1:1; 1:9; and 3:16 notwithstanding."[54] Only K. G. Kuhn among moderns has "flirted with an interpretation like that of Heracleon and Hilgenfeld," writing that

Jn's dualism "divides human beings…into those from God and those from the devil" and that those "from the truth…cannot help but hear" while he "who is below cannot hear at all, cannot believe."[55] After a lengthy review of Old Testament passages, rabbinic exegesis, and the *Apocryphon of John* (a Nag Hammadi tract), Trumbower says that whether any statements in the present text can be safely attributed to a redactor because at cross-purposes with the principal author is "a difficult if not impossible question to answer."[56] The remaining eighty pages of the study, however, constitute such an attempt in a search for traces of an anthropology of fixedness of human natures. He thinks he finds them in the primary evangelist's interpretation of the prologue by adding verses 12c–13 to designate a fixed category explaining why certain persons "born…from God…believed."[57] The Nicodemus and Samaritan woman stories are exegeted to show why he could not believe in Jesus and she could not not believe. And so with other identifications of "fixed origins" in chapters 5–12, the farewell discourses, the passion narrative, and 1 Jn.

Udo Schnelle hoes an easier row in demonstrating the existence of *Antidocetic Christology in the Gospel of John*.[58] In spelling out his method he observes that redaction criticism as used on the Synoptics has not yet adequately been applied to the FG. When it is, it cannot be a matter of theories based on sources that are identified as tradition and redaction viewed as historical or material opposites. It must be seen as the editor's total work on the tradition he received that he incorporated in light of his own theology. Schnelle then goes in search of the antidocetic character of Johannine Christology in Jesus' miracles ("The Visible Christ"), the sacraments ("The Present Christ"), and the prologue ("Christ Incarnate"). A brief concluding chapter locates the position of the Gospel in the Johannine school before the author sums up the opposition to a docetic Christ that his arguments have demonstrated. First written were 2 and 3 John; 1 John then identified an acute controversy with those who would dissolve Jesus of Nazareth into an appearance and deny not only the substance of his being but also the soteriological significance of his cross and resurrection. A detailed theological response to this denial would come only later in the Gospel, which Schnelle argues constituted a conscious polemic against the first docetists. The letters of Ignatius "are very close in content and in time to the Johannine writings" and in them the docetic Christology "is truly palpable for the first time."[59]

Martin Scott tries to show in *Sophia and the Johannine Jews* that Lady Wisdom was as much to the fore in the evangelist's thinking as was the reality of Jesus' humanity.[60] The arguments are by now familiar: The case has been made since J. Rendel Harris (1917) that *logos* (Jn 1:1) might well have been *sophia* but for the fact that a masculine noun was needed for Jesus; *sophia* establishes the female aspect of the divine since the Jewish scriptures conceive of Israel's God as male; the word's gender could not have escaped the fourth evangelist, making "Sophia…the *primary* source for christological reflection at the end of the first century."[61] Chapter 3 attempts to establish the first part of the above statement as fact while the second part is the author's conviction. Assuming both to be true, he examines the way the FG's Christology affected its portrayal of women and served as a "perceptive corrective…to other New Testament writings which stress the subordination of women" (R. E. Brown). Much attention is given to the female in ancient pagan writing and the relation between Wisdom and YHWH in Prov, Sir, and Wis [Sol]. The inescapable lexical gender of *sophia,* however, if Jewish writers in Greek wished to attribute wisdom to Israel's God (the same holds for the feminine *ḥokmah*), means that they had no other choice. Gendered nouns in languages moreover bear little relation to the human sexes. The fact that the Greek *sophia* does not occur in the Johannine corpus would not have strengthened the author's case. He could have written a simpler book on the women of the Johannine Jesus without the linguistic complication. **Richard Cassidy** has been largely engaged in Lukan studies but in turning to *John's Gospel in New Perspective* he explores the sovereignty of Rome and its emperors, especially in relation to the subject Jewish people, moving on to Jesus' sovereign bearing in Jn.[62] This bearing is clearly seen in the performance of his signs/works, in his farewell discourse, his adversaries and Pilate, and in his crucifixion, death, and risen life. Cassidy concludes by asking whether the evangelist could not have consciously cast Jesus in this sovereign role to provide support for the believers of his community under Roman rule.

The special virtue of **Joseph Grassi**'s attempt to learn the identity of "the disciple whom Jesus loved" is that it neatly reports on some English language scholarship on the question previous to the works of Culpepper and Charlesworth.[63] Having done that in brief fashion, he then goes on to conclude from the scanty Gospel data and by resort to some beloved OT figures that the disciple was a Judean highly placed in society (Grassi thinks him "another disciple" of 18:15) who stands as a counterpart to Jesus' affection to Mary Magdalene and as manifestation of the Spirit/Paraclete. The two matters that Grassi does not have sufficient evidence for are the characterization of him as young and his placement near Jesus at the Last Supper as a sign of affection cognate with Jesus' love for children (see Mk 16:13f.).

The anthology compiled by **Mark Stibbe** cited earlier was the fruit of his Nottingham University dissertation on "The Artistry of John." Three other of his titles had a similar origin, of which the first to appear was *John as Storyteller,* followed shortly by *John* in Readings: A New Biblical Commentary, and *John's Gospel.*[64] In the first of these the author calls his method interdisciplinary because of the literary-critical approach employed. Three rather dense chapters explain the vocabulary and intent of modern literary criticism that tends to see a narrative synchronically or as a whole. These are followed by a narrative-historical exposition of Jn 18–19 in five chapters, distinguished perhaps by the opinion that John the Elder is the evangelist and Lazarus the disciple Jesus loved who as eyewitness is the primary source behind part of the Gospel.[65] The technique employed in the second two books is to choose certain narratives like the raising of Lazarus for analysis under the headings plot, time, deep structure, mode, prolepses, narrator, protagonist, minor characters, and source. It is left to modern expositors of lit crit to judge whether Stibbe has mastered the method. As to the category "tradition," he knows what Jn scholarship knows and employs it sparingly. **John Painter**'s *The Quest for the Messiah* is not a commentary although he has written one (1975) but the pursuit of a Johannine theme.[66] He quotes C. H. Dodd with approval: "Messiahship is but the starting point for the evangelist's christology."[67] The quest of the title becomes elusive, however, so detailed is the report on what many scholars have written about many passages. There is no scripture index, but the contents are specific as to the chapters and verses that have any element of the quest for Jesus' identity or person. The Australian scholar ends his book with brief treatments of the quest to arrest Jesus (18:1–11) and the quest for the body (20:1–18), capped by this statement: "The original conclusion of the Gospel (20.30–31) proclaims the Johannine christology as the authentic fulfillment of those expectations and confessions [above mentioned] and all other quests."[68] No attention is paid to chapter 21, perhaps on the theory that at the lakeside the disciples have found in the risen Jesus the Messiah they had long sought. Painter is a careful exegete and deserves to be consulted on any portion of the text about which he has an opinion.

Norman Petersen of Williams College engages in an original study as he explores the "special" language spoken by Jesus and the narrator as contrasted with its meaning in "everyday" language spoken by others in the narrative.[69] The book's title says it will deal with the sociology of light, language, and characterization. The special language is in fact an antilanguage that the speakers of everyday language are portrayed as not comprehending. To give the writer's concluding example: In the everyday language statement that "God loved the world and sent his Son to give it life" is encoded a special language statement "because 'God,' the 'world,' the 'Son,' and 'life' do not for John mean what they do in everyday language." Similarly in 20:31 Jesus' "signs" are not "signs in the everyday Mosaic sense...[and] 'belief'... 'Christ,' 'Son of God,' and 'life' do not mean what they mean in everyday language."[70] (The total and partial misunderstandings thus created are part of Jn's technique to differentiate social groups in both his narrative world and his real world. It remained for **J. Duncan M. Derrett** to do a John book since he had produced works on the Synoptics and a variety of individual New Testament questions. His *The Victim* on the FG's passion narrative finds him familiarly swimming against the scholarly stream.[71] Individual chapters are devoted to eight subjects or themes: Scripture, King, Prophet, Betrayal, Persecution, Power, Passover, and Messiah, "strands [of which] twisted out of long pre-existing ideas"[72] occur before and after chapters 18–19. Derrett's conviction is that Jn has produced a series of typologies derived from scripture corroded somewhat by myth that give the appearance of being historical but are not such and resist any attempt to exegete them critically. "History is a casualty in John, for what we can only call a hierophany takes precedence over it."[73] The Johannine typologies must be acknowledged for what they are, midrashic narratives like those of *TNK* that convey a religious message by image and sustained by metaphor. Jn's direct quotations of this literature number nineteen or eighteen, but his allusions to it are many more. The LXX is more often the source than the MT but also drawn upon are 1 Enoch, 2 Esdras, and the Qumrân scrolls. Derrett is careful to cite the many who have ploughed this ground before him but his thoroughgoing approval is reserved for Rochais (1981) and Moo (1983). He is not gentle with those whose opinions differ from his, most often with blanket dismissals but at times by name and exact citation.

Two Californians, a monk and a professor, have produced meditative reflections on the meaning of the Gospel in the manner of Wijngaards and Dumm. **Bruno Barnhart**[74] is a monk of New Camaldoli at Big Sur, while **L. William Countryman**[75] teaches in the General Theological Union at Berkeley. The first has written a hefty volume that states at the outset that critical scholarship misses the unitive character of Jn, namely, its attempt to bring all reality into one with the Word who is wisdom at its center. Countryman defines mystical union as "an experience of full knowledge of another specific being" and argues that the goal of the union of God and Logos, on whom the believer's union depends, is the mystical union of believing humanity in and with the Father and the Son.

Barnhart engages in pursuit of "a final depth and intensity of meaning." In the patristic manner he sets portions of Jn in relation to the seven days of early Genesis, culminating in the eighth or continuing day. Identifying Jn's basic literary technique as chiastic symmetry, he calls his own approach to the Gospel mandalic, a geometry of the cosmos employed in the Hindu and Buddhist traditions in aid of meditation. Since unity and unification are what this Gospel is about, the author regrets that some Christians need to come on other texts than their own to encounter *lectio divina* for the first time with its invitation to being at one with the One. Examining successive Johannine texts, often in conjunction with Old Testament passages, he sums up the Gospel's core: "The one night of baptismal illumination at the center of our figure [the mandala, from the Sanskrit for circle, with transverse lines crossing at the center] is finally gathered into the unitive light of the one day of the resurrection." A bonus is provided in the penultimate "153 fish" that summarize the FG's main points, some of them pithy in form, others a long paragraph or two. The reader might do well to digest them before launching on this profoundly sacramental book. The much shorter Countryman volume proposes segments of John for reflection entitled Prologue, Conversion, Baptism, Eucharist, Enlightenment, and New Life. In each case it is "the mystic's *experience* of theology that crowns the book [Jn], not intellectual theology." The writer shows himself fully capable of the latter but his primary interest in the believer's experience causes him to leave many historical questions untouched.

R. Alan Culpepper's *John the Son of Zebedee* carries a subtitle that describes the book as the life of a legend.[76] It is refreshing on a number of counts, being a summary of what can be deduced from within the FG, epistles, and Revelation about their respective authors, followed by a lengthy account of the legends that grew about the son of Zebedee from roughly AD 150 to 2000. There are two concluding chapters on reconstructed biographies of John as the author of all five writings (nineteenth century) and critical works on the apostle and his circle or school (twentieth century). Early chapters discuss in detail the fishing industry on the Sea of Galilee, *Boanērges* as probably denoting more than impetuosity of temperament but a designation of prophetic witnesses whose voices would later be heard as from the heavens, and a fairly lengthy examination of who "the disciple Jesus loved" might be. Culpepper concludes that he cannot be the Galilean fisherman but has to be a fairly highly placed Judean who is not one of the Twelve. His candidate is John Mark of Acts 12:12, cousin to Barnabas (Col 4:10), whose name is linked to Peter's in Acts 12:12 and 1 Peter 5:13, and who as "the beloved" appears several times with Peter in the FG (13:23f.; 20:2–8: 21:20–24). Attention is paid to the scant attention paid to the FG up to AD 150 and its embracing by Gnostic Christians thereafter; to which patristic and heretical writers thought it, the epistles, and Revelation to be the work of Zebedee's son and/or the Elder and/or the Seer of Patmos. The development of the tradition is traced from Justin through Irenaeus, by whose time all five writings were thought to be the work of the apostle. The growth of the apostle John legend is recorded in chapters titled "Saint," "Hero," and "Icon." The stories of the unsuccessful attempt to boil him in oil, his final residence in Ephesus, and his part in Mary's dormition/assumption are all told, with a final chapter summarizing dependable modern scholarship on theories of authorship. A bonus is the treatment of the apostle's place in visual art and literature. Altogether, a thoroughly satisfying performance.

Dorothy Lee, an Australian, does a literary study of six long narratives in John that she finds not only symbolic but distinctive, from the overall narrative pattern of the Gospel.[77] These are 2:23—3:36; 4:1–42; 5:1–47; 6; 9; and 11:1—12:11. Her primary concern is their literary structure and reader response to it, but she does not disregard the content of each and its theological implications.

If Culpepper's study was meticulous, **James Charlesworth**'s is even more so on a particular point, *The Beloved Disciple: Whose Witness Validates the Gospel of John?*[78] It is a book of 481 pages that literally turns up every stone going back to Bretschneider (1820) and Baldensperger (1898) on the BD's identity. Boismard thought the unnamed disciple of 1:40 to be Philip (1956) as did Colson (1969), while protagonists of Lazarus are many and Nathanael or Thomas few. The disciple who witnessed Jesus' crucifixion (19:26) is obviously the eyewitness intended in 19:35. When Thomas is told by the others that they have seen the Lord (20:25), he does not need to be told about the wounds in Jesus' hands and side because he alone had witnessed their infliction.[79] After marshalling extensive evidence *pro* and *con* other disciples, Charlesworth reviews the eight criteria that led him to opt for Thomas. They are: *love* (11:16); *anonymity,* beginning in 1:40 and continuing until disclosure in 20:29; *closeness* or authority (seven mentions of Thomas in Jn, only one in Mt, Mk, Lk, and Acts); *lateness* of designation as the "BD" in the unfolding drama; Thomas's willingness to die with Jesus (11:16) leading to his presence at the *cross* (19:26); the *commendation* of the dependable witness by author and editor (19:35; 21:24) with perhaps an early clue planted in 5:32; *fear* at the prospect of *the BD's death* (21:20), that follower on whom Jesus uttered the blessing of 20:29 translated as: "Because you have seen me you have believed. Blessed are those who have not seen and (yet) believe (because of your trustworthiness and valid witness)"; and *Peter,* to whom the BD is almost always portrayed as superior and who is so pejoratively portrayed in chs. 1–20 that a partial rehabilitation had to be achieved in 21.

Charlesworth concedes that no proof of his thesis can ever be possible, "but it has become clear that Thomas is a valid, perhaps the only trustworthy, candidate for the Beloved Disciple."[80]

Craig Koester explores in his *Symbolism in the Fourth Gospel* representative figures (individuals, the crowd, disciples), Jesus' symbolic actions, light and darkness, water, the crucifixion, and symbol and community.[81] Allowing that the FG is written at the level of the evangelist, the author does not employ this as a hermeneutical tool but deals with the symbol system presented by Jn as a narrative of Jesus' actions and utterances. The book's categorization scheme above makes available to preachers and teachers a rich array of Johannine themes and conceits derived equally from Semitic and Graeco-Roman cultures. *John's Wisdom: A Commentary on the Fourth Gospel* is the work of the prolific **Ben Witherington**.[82] It sets out the general character of the various vignettes without exegeting any in great depth, taking the form of a smoothly running narrative like those of Collins and Marrow above. **David Mark Ball** distinguishes, in *"I Am" in John's Gospel,* between sayings without an "image," that is, a predicate, and those with.[83] The sayings in the first case are primarily concerned with Jesus' identity, not his rôle, although both are soteriological.[84] Those with an image, for example, the gate, vine, and living bread, reinforce the use of "I am." Jesus in 4:26 confirms what had been said in the prologue, "that he is the very expression of YHWH."[85] He does not make himself God as his shocked hearers conclude (10:33) nor utter a blasphemy in 8:58f. "From the gospel's point of view it is not Jesus who makes himself God but the reverse....It is the Word...who has made himself flesh."[86]

Quite simply a throwback to nineteenth-century rationalism is **Maurice Casey**'s *Is John's Gospel True?*[87] To be true, he thinks, a gospel must record the works and deeds of Jesus as he spoke or performed them and by this standard the FG fails utterly. Casey takes the paradoxical stand of deploring the demand of some unnamed evangelical contemporaries for literal, historical truth while he himself employs the norm of German and British

Neutestamentlers long dead: Did it, could it, have happened as described? When the historical reality of Jesus' activities is given in the Synoptics, Jn departs from it, resorting to much composition by a later church. As part of his argument, there was no Aramaic substrate for this Greek Gospel. (Casey confidently gives the English of Mk's Aramaic original). The FG community in Ephesus was a group debarred from attending Jewish meetings because it had acquired a Gentile identification, with many beliefs and practices remote from the Jesus of history. The actual Jesus tradition was rewritten to meet the needs of the Jn community, a technique often adopted by ancient authors. A glaring example is the account of Jesus' trial before Pilate and death. The risen-life accounts contain many more elaborations on actuality. No record remains of the disciples pointing out to disbelievers the rock tomb for criminals in which Jesus was buried, for Casey a requirement for belief in his bodily resurrection. The FG is profoundly untrue, anti-Jewish, and with its claim of the divinity of Jesus "infringes Jewish monotheism."

To track Jn's dependence on the Jewish scriptures, **Maarten J. J. Menken**[88] conducts eleven distinct textual studies that explore the following seventeen texts: 1:23; 2:17; 6:31; 6:45; 12:15; 12:40; 13:18; 15:25; 19:36; 19:37; 7:38; 7:42; 8:17; 10:34; 12:34; 12:38; 19:24. All are introduced by a phrase like "the prophet said" or "so it is written." There are many allusions to the OT besides that are not thus signaled. Most of the quotations do not agree in exact wording with the LXX but the majority come from it and not from any other Greek version or the Hebrew. The two exceptions to the latter are 12:40 and 13:18, which may be Jn's translation of the Hebrew. Following any one or even several of Maarten's rich sleuthings will bring new respect for the genius of the evangelist as master of his people's scriptures. **Paul N. Anderson** of Oregon's George Fox University (Society of Friends) examines the Christology of the FG through the lens of chapter 6.[89] He sets himself to analyze the terrain and at times contradiction that mark Jesus' Bread of Life discourse—according to

Bultmann the unity and disunity present there. Anderson holds that theological, literary, and historical interests have motivated all previous analysis; he intends his to be epistemological. Four chapters are devoted to the search for unity and disunity by exploring the relation of sign to discourse, the dialectical character of the latter, and whether 6:51c–58 shows the writer to be a sacramentalist or antisacramentalist. Anderson does not identify the passage as an interpolation but thinks Bultmann correct in finding an "apparent contradiction between the christology of the evangelist and the sacramentality represented by [these verses]."[90] Calling on the letters of Ignatius and the known secessionism described in 1 Jn, Anderson finds in Jn 6 objection to "institutionalizing attempts to centralize the church [and]…the rise of ordinance motifs,… [understanding] the power of faith in Jesus Christ to be better expressed in relational and familial ways than in ritual ones."[91] Such opposition to an institutional trend would seem, however, to leave Jn a non-Ignatian rather than an anti-Ignatian by his silences. The dialectical approach to Christology found in the chapter seems to have arisen out of the existentializing (Anderson's term) of events from Jesus' life, primarily his signs, and "the interpretation of Christocentric encounters with God, which the evangelist must have experienced."[92] Three segments of Jn are carefully exegeted, 6:1–24; 25–66; and 67–71. The author concludes that there is a modified synchronic approach calculated to reveal three levels of dialectical tension: between the evangelist and his tradition, between his literary means and his audience, and between socio-religious factors and his Christology. Anderson's exegesis of 51c–58[93] needs to be read with care to see if he is in search of Jn's meaning or discovers one he is committed to. "Despite the mention of 'eating,' and Jesus' 'flesh' given for the life of the world, the reference is clearly to Jesus' *death on the cross,* not primarily the eucharist." Can Jesus' followers "'drink the cup' of suffering and eat the bread (of affliction) offered by the Son of Man?" A good question, but does the passage suggest it?

A study by **Derek Tovey,** a New Zealander, spells out the narrative art of the implied author, who is a disciple of Jesus, as close to the events as the FG's characters identified by name, and one who shares the BD's perspective.[94] The events reported on are based on eyewitness and firsthand reports by a narrator theologically informed on their meaning by the hindsight the Paraclete's assistance has afforded him. This evangelist can go abruptly from telling a tale of figures in a story to adopting an authorial omniscient perspective. In sum, Tovey provides the reader with a detailed analysis of what Franz Mussner calls John's "mode of vision." **J. M. Ford** of the University of Notre Dame prepares for her study of the theology of salvation in Jn, which she sees expressed in the Father's motherly love for the Son transmitted as friendship for humanity, by exploring in depth models of salvation/redemption in the patristic and medieval periods, the Jewish scriptures and the rabbis, and modern figures like Unamuno and Moltmann.[95] Throughout, the *pathos* of God is seen through the image of the mother as sufferer. Like Forestell, Nicholson, and others, she finds no redemption by blood in John. She identifies, rather, a soteriology of Jesus' descent and ascent in which, out of the love of friendship, he will take his friends back to the Father with him. Friendship is the leitmotiv of the FG: the Father's love for the Son and for the disciples because they have loved Jesus, the Son's love for his friends, including Lazarus and the unnamed BD, and the Jesus who loves his life but will lose it. Discipline among ideas eludes Ford somewhat in her treatment of the prologue, where she relies heavily on *sophia* while disregarding *logos*. There are many insightful treatments of the feminine in this work: God's motherly love for us, Jesus' tenderness in the foot washing of the disciples, and the love expressed in the Last Supper discourse that transcends gender.

Jey Kanagaraj is an Indian whose academic dissertation was done at Durham University.[96] In its attempt to relate Jesus' intimate communion with God to Merkabah mysticism (the celestial chariot of Ezek 1:15–21), it neglects to indicate that as part of the *Hekhalot* literature (heavenly palaces), the provenance is third to seventh century CE Babylon. The attention given to the writings of Jesus' contemporary Philo, postbiblical apocalyptic literature, and Qumrân finds the author on solider ground. When he turns to the descent-ascent and light motifs in Jn and to the sending of the Son and the divine indwelling, all are surprisingly short of parallels with the Jewish mysticism texts. A reference to Jn 12:41, where the evangelist says that Isaiah saw the Lord's glory, and other motifs of seeing and glory in the FG are the slender threads on which a claim of influence by a pervasive Jewish mysticism hangs.

Bruce Malina and **Richard Rohrbaugh** bring us into another world entirely, that of the societal matrix of John's Gospel.[97] They forgo making critical comments on passages or verses, although in many observations made in passing they show familiarity with the technique. Instead they opt for examining each pericope in turn from the viewpoints of the cultural and linguistic anthropology of life in the ancient Graeco-Roman and Palestinian Jewish societies. The results are a number of insights not to be found in the best of commentaries. The in-group that framed the FG was an antisociety with its own antilanguage, for example, "glory" for honor in an honor-shame society, "world" *(kosmos)* for the larger Israelite society, and "purity/uncleanness" for boundary markers between the ordered and the disordered in the human body. The reader is challenged to come abreast of the terms "high-context" society, in which, for example, all are aware of agricultural methods and vocabulary, and "low-context" society, those of our contemporaries, for example, who have mastered computer language or theater talk like a *"noir* comedy." The sociological technique once established, it is used consistently to explain terms and events in the evangelist's day that are taken to be the same as in Jesus' day. John's *hoi Ioudaîoi* are translated "the Judeans" throughout without further discussion. The influence on this Gospel of the Hebraic collective personality, kinship and fictive families (that is, of associates), and mother and father to son, and family to nonfamily relationships are all explored. So, too, are the marriage and burial customs of the age, institutions like social banditry and the charge against Barabbas (18:40), and the bodily "zones of purposeful action" in a description of the foot washing.[98] In every case passages from pagan classical authors, the Mishnah, and the much later Talmuds are drawn on to give a picture of the culture and customs of the age. At times the reader who is a layperson in sociology may feel that an iron form is being imposed on successive FG data, especially when honor/reputation and shame/disgrace are alleged as the motivations good and bad for the actions of its characters. On balance, however, the book provides a lively learning experience.

The Lawsuit Motif in the Fourth Gospel is the sub-title of **Andrew Lincoln**'s primarily literary but also historical and theological exercise.[99] He views the narrative of Jesus' appearance before Pilate and "the Jews" (18:19–24) as a cosmic trial in which God passes a verdict on Jesus, who in turn acts as witness and judge before Pilate to supply "the decisive clue to the whole of history from within its midst."[100] A theology of the event prevails in the four concluding reflections that name God's decisive verdict as the outcome of the trial, namely, Jesus' death and resurrection which are the causes of the life of the world. There is built into these faith-based remarks a mild polemic against "Christian scholars who would claim to be simply descriptive exegetes"[101] in their inattention to the trial's cosmic significance. **Tom Thatcher**'s concern, after having distinguished between written and oral forms of speech and established four criteria for the riddle, is whether the thirty-eight sayings of Jesus in Jn that meet the test could have been remembered as spoken in that form or were Johannine constructs.[102] Chapters 13–17 are described as a "riddling session." Three chapters are devoted to the various dramatic, mission, and salvation riddles, shedding some light on cryptic sayings that have stumped exegetes. Intended to be riddles spoken to riddlees who did not have enough knowledge to comprehend them, they were understood by hearers aided by group logic, hearers distinguished by what they "know"; thus, for example, 4:32; 6:51; 11:25f.; 12:32; 13:10. The concern of **Marianne Meye Thompson** in *The God of the Gospel of John*[103] is to challenge the theological assumption concerning Jn that it is "routinely read as a narrowly Christological and, even more acutely, 'Christocentric Gospel,'"[104] whereas in fact it is profoundly theocentric. The corrective she supplies takes its rise from Jn's use of God as "Father" about 120 times and "God" 108 times. God is supremely the possessor of life (5:26) and a Father known to Jesus and made known by him, whose life-giving power is the Spirit conveyed through the Son. God is the object of worship through Jesus; Jesus is not directly its object. A brief concluding chapter states that "the character of God in the narrative remains only indirectly accessible to the reader," made known by his words and embodied in his deeds. C. K. Barrett is quoted: "God is known and God's presence felt only because the Son alone 'presents' God to the world, is wholly transparent to God, and is the only reliable vehicle for God's presence and action in the world"; and John Ashton: "What the divine agent 'heard' from God is disclosed not in his words but in his life; the 'what' is displayed in the 'how.'"[105]

Ford Larsson goes in a different direction in *God in the Fourth Gospel,* telling the reader in his subtitle that it will be about Jn's treatment of God in a number of landmark figures in theology.[106] Luther's preaching on John in 1528–40 resulted in almost 2,000 printed pages fleshed out by disciples. Larsson identifies twelve traits of God discoverable there, of which being "for us" is primary but also stresses God's triune reality and self-expression in Christ. Calvin's 616-page commentary on Jn gives seven traits or attributes while taking pains to avoid "trifles of metaphysics" (Calvin). God is one who is hidden and revealed in that Gospel, active and provident, loving, a securer of stability, a promoter of obedience and order. John's God betrays the predestinatory traits in certain chapters but no outspoken predestination to condemnation. If 1:12 seems to proclaim man's free will, verse 13 refutes it. The Swedish theologian in a major leap down to

Westcott (1901), Holtzmann (1910), Bultmann (1976), and Brown (1998) enumerates the qualities of deity identified by each in his interpretation of Jn. They are what might be expected with a few exceptions such as Holtzmann's naming suffering as a trait of God and Bultmann's describing God as one who gives offense. Brown alone "seems not to find the question important." In 300 pages of commentary he confronts the idea of God only when it surfaces in the prologue, the "I am," and the "glory" passages. Elsewhere God is seen as self-revealed in uttering a *logos* and, as the occasion warrants, is found to be true, spirit, holy, just, living, and greater than the Son. Overall, Larsson seems to have fished all night and come up with a thoroughly predictable catch, but in the process he spreads a rich table of theological history.

Mark Matson's Duke University dissertation under D. Moody Smith is a text study of Luke 22–24 to see if it is influenced by Jn. He entitles it *In Dialogue with Another Gospel?*[107] A first chapter reviews the Luke-John relation as explored by Schniewind (1914), Neirynck (1979), Dauer (1972), and Soards (1987). Matson concludes that Luke 22:34, 67; 24:12, 36 bear a striking similarity to John and that when Luke reorders Markan events as in 22:31–34, 67–68, and 23:2–4, there is verbal agreement with John. Moreover, when Luke differs from Mark, the passage displays Johannine features (for example, 22:47–53). In those cases Luke's narrative stands midway between Mark and John. Despite these and a number of other connections, they are not enough to establish a literary relation. Matson concludes: "If Luke used John, that use took place alongside his use of Mark, and the result was an admixture of sources together with Lukan shaping and modification."

Demetrius Dumm's *A Mystical Portrait of Jesus* has a title that resembles that of Kanagaraj, but the two are dissimilar in content except for the obvious citation of most of the same passages.[108] Twelve brief chapters with titles like "The Hour Has Come," "Testifying to the Truth," and "That They May Be One" employ texts from the Gospel as subheadings, none in their sequence there but as they pertain to the theme of the chapter heading. The author's comments follow each quoted text in a marriage of piety and scholarship of the sort found in Professor O'Day's "Reflections." Dumm, a monk of St. Vincent Archabbey, credits two recent writers as major contributors to his thinking, L. William Countryman and **Sandra Schneiders**.[109] The latter, a practiced exegete, observes in concert with Andrew Lincoln above that modern biblical interpretation has become "a strictly academic pursuit of historical knowledge that regards any personal involvement of the teacher with the subject matter of the text as, at best, a distraction and, at worst, a failure of academic rigor."[110] She hopes to return to fifteen earlier centuries of biblical interpretation with chapters such as "Commitment in the New Testament," warning against seeking one's own glory; the Lazarus narrative in "The Community of Eternal Life," enabling readers to integrate "the ever-ambiguous experiences of death, that of loved ones and their own, into their faith vision"; and "a Community of Friends" on the foot washing as an invitation less to thoughts of self-humiliation or service than to contemplating a reversal of superior and inferior in the social order.

Adele Reinhartz accepts the invitation to personal involvement with the text in her anguished *Befriending the Beloved Disciple*.[111] In her earlier book she had not identified herself as a Jew but followed the rules of dispassionate scholarship to find in Jn a "cosmic tale." The autobiographical prologue to this book tells of her keeping her ethnic identity so undisclosed that it reached her ears that one student had said to another, "I think she's a Catholic nun." Now, like Jeremiah, she can keep her anger in no longer. The BD who is identified by the evangelist as the authenticator of all that has been written is her target. She wishes him to be a friend but concludes she cannot.[112] Her judgment on his "historical and ecclesiological tales," whatever the situation of the community he speaks for, is that his "Gospel marginalizes the Johannine Jews, a group with which I identify."[113] His major offense in the writer's eyes is that he requires belief in Jesus as Messiah and Son of God, consigning those who cannot believe to rejection by God and figurative death. In tracking the unacceptable exclusivity of the FG and compliance in it by "followers of the Beloved Disciple then and now,"[114] Reinhartz's critical study finds no comfort in theories of a "family feud" in the Jn community, the two-level theory of life in a community that drew on incidents in Jesus' life, or the supposition that *Ioudaîoi* referred to Judeans rather than the whole people. For her, "the Jews" in its more than seventy uses in Jn is a term of obloquy and never once describes members of the BD's group, despite its occasional neutral or favorable usages. The historical tale embedded in it has the only violent acts reported in it done by Jews. Judas the betrayer is *Ioudas,* that is, "a Jew." (There is no advertence to the other member of the Twelve of that name; see Mk 6:31; Lk 6:16; Jude 1). The desire of this people to kill Jesus and plot Lazarus's death qualifies them as offspring of the devil. This book is a cry of the heart that conveys the anguish the Jews have experienced for centuries in the way that term has appeared in the FG and been understood by Christians to mean for as many centuries. Paradoxically, the author sets aside her considerable critical skills to determine what might have been going on in the ethnically Jewish Jn community to account for this usage, totally unusual to us, somewhat like saying repeatedly of racial segregation, cross burnings, and other expressions of racial hatred that "the Americans" had done all this. Which "Jews" are Jn's "Jews" is a question that needs attacking, even though discovering the answer would do nothing to reverse centuries of Christian persecution of that people.

An older study than the several cited immediately above is the work of **François Vouga**.[115] It sets itself to answer questions like those that ask to whom the FG is addressed, for whom it was written, and what it wishes to bring to the mind of its intended readers. The root of the problem is that the destruction of the Temple and a restructured Israel on the lines of Pharisee interpretation of the Law had produced a Judaism quite different from that of Jesus' day. The unlikely alliance of the Pharisees and Temple priests in the earlier period is not the least of the anomalies Vouga identifies in the text of Jn. If the various villains of the piece are ciphers for certain opponents of the John community, how explain the disappearance of "the Jews" from 14–17 and in their place the many warnings to the disciples of confrontation by "the world"? These chapters receive a verse-by-verse exegesis, with special attention to the meaning of the world's hatred that the community is told to expect (15:18—16:4a). It will be based on a hatred for (15:23) and ignorance of (16:3) the Father and the Son, all of it characterized as sin. Three hypotheses are presented, one of which may explain what is meant by the world's hatred: (1) that the community continues to be the target of a pagan anti-Judaism of long standing; (2) that it is the target of imperial absolutism; (3) and that the Christian communities of Asia Minor are feeling the scrutiny and the whip of empire, not directly but in the towns and provinces. They are being both warned and consoled by the FG. The terms "the world" and "the Jews" are not equivalent in this Gospel. Rather, they envision two different situations, the hostility of a segment of Judaism and the persecuting activity of Domitian. Obviously there were polemical exchanges between the former and a community committed to the unique divine sonship of Jesus, but Jn's intent is not primarily polemical. "The gospel of John is a writing concerned with a struggle *for the truth and against discouragement,* for hanging on against giving up." Vouga cites Dauer on the point that the exchange with Pilate is meant to underscore the political innocence of incipient Christianity.[116] John finds hope in recalling the history of Jesus, using that history to fashion a prophetic word. The word-event made flesh becomes the principle of a critical rereading of the history of the tradition and its present. The Johannine community, finding its roots in its people's history (4:22b), reports on the debates with Judaism as no cause for surprise, for in them Israel faced with "the Jews" is finding its identity.

The best wine has been saved for the last. **John Ashton**'s *Understanding the Fourth Gospel* stands out among all the works of FG scholarship in English of the 1990s, a judgment in which

Lindars, Meeks, and Lloyd Gaston concur (sic jacket).[117] He thinks that Bultmann, "unmatched in learning, breadth, and understanding, towers like a colossus. Nevertheless...every answer [he] gives to the really important questions he raises—is wrong." The layman long at Marburg was right to name as Jn's main theme that Jesus was a revealer, but his revelation was *that* he revealed, nothing more. Ashton devotes his first three chapters to a report on Jn scholarship before Bultmann, by Bultmann, and after Bultmann. Two nuggets from the first period were the speculation of Karl Bretschneider in 1820 that the controversies between Jesus and Pharisees were actually between Christians and Jews in the second century, and M. von Aberle's 1861 discussion (a first) of the inserted "Blessing against Heretics (Minim)" in a context of Jn's repudiation of charges against the early community. Karl Bornhäuser was also prescient when, in 1928, he concluded that the word *Ioudaîoi* could not be identified simply with the Jews of Judea but might better describe "Torah fanatics who are at the same time *inquisitors* whose job it is to watch over the Law and to rectify and punish any infringement" (*Das Johannesevangelium,* p. 141).

A chapter entitled "Religious Dissent" attempts to situate the Johannine Christians among the numerous dissenters of the age "when Judaism as we know it was still in its infancy."[118] Ashton's tentative conclusion is that "the Jews" is the self-designation of the powerful party—a coalition of the priestly caste that had lost its raison d'être with the destruction of the Temple and the very influential Pharisees—that was busy trying to stamp out views it regarded as subversive. The Johannine group, which names "the chief priests and the Pharisees" as its antagonists (7:32; 11:47, 57; 18:3), not the Pharisees alone, could well have been one of their targets. As to a large group calling itself "the Jews" where everyone was Jewish, Ashton summons the witness of Josephus, who speaks of the returned sixth-century exiles of the south as *Ioudaîoi* in contrast to the Judeans who stayed behind, the Samaritans, and other northerners not enthusiastic for Temple worship (*Antiquities* xi.173 and xi. 340–46, in which Shechem, modern Nablus, is mentioned as inhabited by expellees from Jerusalem charged with violating the dietary laws, the Sabbath regulations, or "any other such sin"). If the Oxford scholar's speculation is correct, there would have been violent harassment by the "the Jews" of the Jn community, to which they responded with the verbal violence of the Gospel. See 8:48 for the charge that Jesus was a Samaritan and attempts to stone (v. 59) or even kill him (v. 40), one of the five places that speak of "the Jews'" desire to do so, where "Jesus" is a surrogate for the much later community.

Ashton wonders whether the evangelist might not have been a member of an Essene group early in life, for "he had dualism in his bones."[119] Brown and Schnackenburg espouse a theory of indirect dependence on the Dead Sea community while Bultmann goes further to suggest that he was a convert from Gnosticism. Ashton for his part thinks this would "account for the dualism of the Gospel and for its strange new Christology."[120] There is a lengthy chapter on the title "Messiah" and shorter ones on "Son of God" and "Son of Man" as all three are used by John and the Synoptics. Identifying the first 377 pages of discussions in part 2 of his book, "Genesis," as historical, he turns to part 3, "Revelation," terming it exegetical. The meaning of the FG or its grand conception is the story of its origins, although separable from it. That meaning is a theology of revelation. Jesus' task is to do the Father's will, which is essentially to establish God's glory.[121] Chapters entitled "Departure and Return," "Passion and Resurrection," and the final "The Medium and the Message" convey the Gospel as revelation, which says almost nothing of the content of the revelation. A divine envoy is charged with carrying it to the world, the object of God's salvific love. Those who accept the revelation are granted the life of the new age. While Jesus' true home is in heaven, the only heavenly mysteries revealed to him by God are those disclosed in his own life and death. God's plan for the world is transcribed in terms of a human life. The "what" is displayed in the "how."

Ashton brought out eight previously published or delivered papers three years after his *Understanding* to refine certain points made there.[122] He finds the prologue to be a case of Wisdom's role as God's agent that has been taken over, adapted, and made to function as a myth. Now purely Christian, it tries to "make sense of the community's rejection by the Jews" as it relives the experience undergone by the Revealer. The term *Ioudaîoi* has taken on an allegorical or symbolic function, whatever its original denotation. It cannot mean the Jewish leaders, since all the opportunities to use *archontes* have been passed over. As maintained in the book cited above, it may have been remotely historical for the returned Judean exiles who held Moses to be their great one and were contemptuous of "the people of the land" collectively.[123] This would include the Galileans and Samaritans. In wrestling with the problem of how "newness" entered the Jewish world as represented by claims of Jesus' equality with God (5:18, 30; 10:30; 19:7), Ashton proposes as the origin of the concept the heavenly messenger of numerous OT passages. Justin Martyr a half-century after Jn held that the voice saying from the burning bush "I am that I am" was that of an angel, not of God.[124] As to how the bridge came to be crossed from claims for Jesus back to Daniel, Ezekiel, and Exodus, Ashton says he is at a loss to hypothesize. He is not hesitant to repudiate his formerly held position that the FG was produced in a number of successive editions. Rather, he thinks it done by one author over a long period with the distinct possibility, not the certainty, that it was the result of two editions. In any case, it was "a work of charismatic prophecy discernible in the Johannine community."[125] The only vigorous polemic of the book is directed at those protagonists of narrative criticism, who would say that the historical criticism of Jn can be dispensed with, that is, that all we need to do is examine the story before us. It is a narrative, to be sure, but we learn much about it by analyzing all the elements it contains that might have contributed to it.

Many have observed the spiral rather than the linear character of Jn's rhetoric, others a succession of chiastic structures throughout. A Norwegian scholar engaged in a pastorate, **Gunnar Østenstad** sees a series of concentric structures in which the elements are arranged around a common center.[126] He plots the following seven sections after the prologue, each having as many as five sequences or as few as one: 1:19—2:25; 3:1—4:54; 5:1—7:52; 8:12—12:50; 13:1—17:26; 18:1—19:42; 20:1—21:25, encompassing twenty five sequences. The center verse in each sequence is the important one that, if designated C, is flanked by A, B, and B[1], A[1], or D by A, B, C, and C[1], B[1], and A[1]. Jesus as the New Temple is the main theme of the FG, God's presence on earth in the person of the Son of Man. A way to come abreast of the book's thesis is to identify the central verse in all twenty five sequences, then see if the verses leading up to it are matched in content by those that follow it. Østenstad provides numerous charts to help the reader see at a glance what he is convinced is the architectonic principle of the Gospel. To illustrate: The five sequences within section 5 in chapter 13 reveal Jesus' love for his disciples as the center of the section, while each of the two sequences before and after it will be characterized by a central theme of its own, namely, Judas identified as a betrayer matched by Judas as a son of perdition. It is not news that biblical writings like certain psalms and wisdom's house built on seven pillars (Prv 9:1) are constructed artfully. The question for us to ask is this: Did Jn have the scheme that this writer deduces?

An American and a Japanese, feminist scholars **Adeline Fehribach**, SCN,[127] and **Satoko Yamaguchi**[128] have respectively dealt with the female characters in Jn and two in particular, to conclude that what is written there should reconfirm Christian women in their role and reveal men guilty of dominance of women from the postapostolic age onward in their interpretation of biblical texts. Fehribach finds in Jesus, the messianic bridegroom of all the women in Jn including his mother,[129] a symbolism that may not have occurred to the evangelist. For Yamaguchi the Bethany scene (13:1–44) depicts Martha as a leader in ministry by serving (12:2; cf. Lk 10:40), while Mary's anointing of Jesus' feet anticipates the foot washing. Certain internal conflicts in the community may be reflected in the downplaying of the sisters' ministerial and leadership roles.

James L. Resseguie employs the now-familiar technique of narrative theory to explore point of view, rhetoric, persons, actions, and plot in the FG as a means to lay bare its art and artifice.[130] For **Terry Griffith** the "new look" of his title is directed at the "idols" of 1 Jn 5:21, which he takes to be the continuing cultic practices of the writer's fellow Jews.[131] **Dorothy Lee**'s more recent book views the symbolism of Jn as neither arbitrary nor decorative but intrinsic to revelation.[132] Her iconic reading is of Jesus's flesh, living water, the vine, God as Father, motherhood, darkness, anointing, resurrection, and life. **Margaret M. Beirne** dismisses the gender-pairings of Lk and Lk-Acts as not her concern, contrasting with them such examples of equality of discipleship in Jn as Jesus' mother and the royal official, Nicodemus and the Samaritan women, the blind man and Martha.[133] Readers must determine whether this narrative reconstruction describes the evangelist's intent. The detailed study of **Charles E. Hill** challenges the scholarly commonplace that the FG was early found suspect for its Gnostic orientation and rescued as Catholic only in the second century by St. Irenaeus and others.[134] Braun (1959), Hengel (1989), and Kieffer (1992) are the contemporaries who swam against the stream. In the thoroughly satisfying *Ingesting Jesus: Eating and Drinking in the Gospel of John,* Canadian scholar **Jane S. Webster** examines all the FG references to foodstuffs and eating, drinking, or ingesting them in the ordinary way and the consuming process as metaphor.[135] Her careful treatment of the latter inspires confidence in her exegesis of each passage (even to "Zeal for your house will consume me" and the "tasting death" of those who do not keep Jesus' word). **Mary L. Coloe** sees Jesus as the Temple in the FG, hence God's dwelling place among us now in the living Temple of the Christian community.[136]

Notes

Introduction

1. Like the present writer's *John*: Interpretation: A Commentary for Teachers and Preachers (Atlanta, 1988).

1. The Landmark Commentaries

1. See Arnold Ehrhardt, "The Gospels in the Muratorian Fragment," in *The Framework of the New Testament Stories* (Cambridge, 1964), 19, which provides the Latin text; full English text in Bruce Metzger, *The Canon of the New Testament: Its Origin, Development, and Significance* (Oxford, 1987), 305–7.

2. *The History of the Church,* 3.39. ·

3. Metzger, 55.

4. 1 *Apology,* 66.3; *Dialogue with Trypho,* 103.8.

5. 1 *Apol.,* 46.2; *Dial.,* 105.1.

6. 1 *Apol.,* 61.4, an apparent quotation of Jn 3:3, 5.

7. *Dial.,* 81.4.

8. See Metzger, 150.

9. See Elaine Pagels, *The Johannine Gospel in Gnostic Exegesis: Heracleon's Commentary on John* (Nashville and New York, 1971), 86–88.

10. *Adv. Haer.,* 3.1.1f., quoted in Eusebius, *H.C.,* 5.8.

11. Quoted in Eusebius, *H.C.*, 6.14.7.

12. E. C. Hoskyns, ed. [posthumously by] F. N. Davey, *The Fourth Gospel* (London, 1940, 1947).

13. Rudolf Bultmann, *The Gospel of John* (Göttingen, 1941; English translation, Philadelphia, 1971).

14. C. K. Barrett, *The Gospel according to St. John* (London, 1955; Philadelphia, 1978).

15. C. H. Dodd, *The Interpretation of the Fourth Gospel* (Cambridge, 1953); *Historical Tradition in the Fourth Gospel* (Cambridge, 1963).

16. Rudolf Schnackenburg, *The Gospel according to John,* 3 vols. (Freiburg, 1965–75; English translation, New York, 1968–82).

17. Raymond E. Brown, *The Gospel according to John,* Doubleday Anchor Bible 29 and 29A (Garden City, 1966–70).

18. F.-M. Braun, *Jean le théologien,* 2 vols. (Paris, 1959–64).

19. Barnabas Lindars, *The Gospel of John* (London, 1972).

20. Ernst Haenchen, *John,* 2 vols. (Tübingen, 1980; English translation, Philadelphia, 1984). The bibliography in vol. 2, 254–346, the work of translator-editor Robert W. Funk and editor Ulrich Busse, is superb.

21. Robert Kysar, *The Fourth Evangelist and His Gospel* (Minneapolis, 1975); "The Fourth Gospel: A Report on Recent Research," *Aufstieg und Niedergang der Römischer Welt,* ed. H. Temporini and W. Haase (Berlin, 1985), II/3, 2389–2480. Reviewed are more than 400 books and articles of 290 authors, the latest dated 1977. Another 66 authors in works published 1977–83 are listed in "The Gospel of John in Current Research," *Religious Studies Review* 9, 4 (1983): 314–23. See also Edward Malatesta, *St. John's Gospel: 1920–1965* (Rome, 1967), and Hartwig Thyen, "Aus der Literatur zum Johannesevangelium," *Theologische Rundschau* 39 (1974) and 42 (1977).

22. Wilbert Francis Howard, *The Fourth Gospel in Recent Criticism and Interpretation,* rev. C. K. Barrett (London, 1955).

23. See n. 12 above.

24, Hoskyns and Davey, 84.

25. Ibid., 163.

26. Ibid., 122.

27. Bultmann, 16; 17, n. 5.

28. Ibid., 43; see also 47, 53, 81 for the self-understanding that man constantly seeks and that constantly eludes him except for the absolute revelation in Jesus, which alone makes it possible to see himself as he is before God.

29. Ibid., 67, n. 2; see also p. 83.

30. Kysar, 14.

31. Bultmann, 84–85.

32. Ibid., 85.

33. Ibid.

34. Ibid., 111.

35. Ibid., 461.

36. A. Faure, "Die alttestamentliche Zitate in 4. Evangelium und Quellenscheidungshypothese," *Zeitschrift für die neutestamentliche Wissenschaft* 21 (1922): 107ff.

37. Kysar, 26–27. The authors are R. Schnackenburg, op. cit.; Jürgen Becker, "Wunder und Christologie," *New Testament Studies* 16 (1969–70): 130–48; Robert T. Fortna, *The Gospel of Signs: A Reconstruction of the Narrative Source Underlying the Fourth Gospel* (Cambridge, 1970); W. Nicol, *The Sēmeia in the Fourth Gospel* (Brill, 1972); Howard M. Teeple, *The Literary Origin of the Gospel of John* (Evanston, 1974).

38. See Bultmann, 111. The translator of this book, George R. Beasley-Murray, has produced an exhaustive commentary of his own of high quality, *John,* Word Biblical Commentary 36 (Waco, 1987).

39. (London, 1955; 1978).

40. Barrett (1978), 26.

41. Ibid., 40.

42. Ibid., 39.

43. Ibid., 74.

44. Ibid., 89, 91.

45. See ibid., 583–87.

46. Ibid., 120; in *The Gospel of John and Judaism* (Philadelphia, 1975), the Franz Delitzsch Lectures written in German and translated by D. M. Smith, Barrett concluded that Jn combines Gnosis and anti-Gnosticism, apocalyptic and nonapocalyptic material, Judaism and anti-Judaism, all in a theological synthesis based on a dialectic between love and *gnōsis,* in the historical situation in which John finds himself.

47. See n. 15 above.

48. Ibid.

49. Dodd, *Interpretation,* 444–53.

50. Ibid., 445.

51. Dodd, *Historical Tradition,* 348, 349.

52. Ibid., 424–25.

53. Ibid., 426.

54. Ibid., 150. On pp. 28–30 he provides such a schema, opting against a literary dependence of Jn and in favor of "all four evangelists [having] felt themselves to be bound by a pre-canonical tradition in which the broad lines of the story were already fixed" (p. 30).

55. Ibid., 115. Such is the conclusion of a number of contemporary scholars who question whether the total nonimplication of Jesus in the political events in Roman Palestine, as reported by the evangelists, can have been true to the facts.

56. Ibid., 123.

57. Ibid., 172.

58. Ibid., 194.

59. Ibid., 232.

60. Ibid., 300.

61. Ibid., 386–87.

62. Ibid., 420.

63. Ibid., 428.

64. Ibid.

65. See Paul Achtemeier, "Omne Verbum Sonat: The New Testament and the Oral Environment of Late Western Antiquity," *Journal of Biblical Literature* 109, 1 (1990): 3–27.

66. Brown, *The Gospel according to John* (xiii–xxi), Anchor Bible 29A (Garden City, N.Y.: Doubleday, 1970), 1080–82.

67. Ibid., p. C.

68. Ibid.

69. Ibid., p. CI.

70. Ibid., 23.

71. Ibid., p. LXXI.

72. Ibid., p. LXXII.

73. Ibid., p. LXXIV.

74. See ibid., 374, n. 22. By vol. 29A, 691, this has been modified to Jn's "referring to the Synagogue in general and fighting a policy that is, at least, in effect in all the synagogues of the area he knows."

75. See, for example, his positing of four independent sources for Jn 20:10, resulting in vv. 1–2, 3–10; 11:13; 14–18 (which had two other independent forms, Mk 10:9–11 and Mt 28:9–10), in *John (xii–xxi)* 29A, 998–1004.

76. See n. 16 above; the three volumes cover a little over 1,700 pages.

77. Schnackenburg, vol. 1, 46–47.

78. Ibid., 47.

79. Ibid., 43.

80. Ibid., 101–4.

2. The Question of Sources

1. Eugen Ruckstuhl, *Die literarische Einheit des Johannesevangeliums* (Fribourg/Switz., 1951). Eduard Schweizer, *Egō Eimi* (Göttingen, 1939), had held a similar position on its stylistic unity, which he modified somewhat in a second edition (1965).

2. Wilhelm Wilkens, *Die Entstehung des vierten Evangeliums* (Zollikon, 1958); he has not departed from his original position in *Zeichen und Werke* (Zürich, 1969). Later studies in tradition and redaction were done by W. Nicol of South Africa, *The Sēmeia in the Fourth Gospel* (Leiden, 1972), and Howard M. Teeple, *The Literary Origin of the Gospel of John* (Evanston, 1974). Using form analysis, Nicol showed how the miracle stories in the signs source are to be separated out from Jn. Teeple posited a signs source (SA) and a semi-Gnostic, Hellenistic mysticism source, mostly of discourses (G). These were edited into a gospel by the evangelist (E) whose work was subsequently recast by a redactor (R).

3. D. Moody Smith, *The Composition and Order of the Fourth Gospel: Bultmann's Literary Theory* (New Haven and London, 1965).

4. Robert Tomson Fortna, *The Gospel of Signs: A Reconstruction of the Narrative Source Underlying the Fourth Gospel* (London, 1970).

5. Ibid., 2.

6. Ibid., 217.

7. See ibid., 223.

8. See ibid., 225.

9. Robert Tomson Fortna, *The Fourth Gospel and Its Predecessor: From Narrative Source to Present Gospel* (Philadelphia, 1988).

10. Ibid., 30, 34, and see 35, n. 61.

11. Urban C. von Wahlde, *The Earliest Version of John's Gospel: Recovering the Gospel of Signs* (Wilmington, 1989).

12. Ibid., Appendix A, 190–91, where they are listed. In ch. 3, pp. 66–155, they are scrutinized and defended.

13. M. C. White, *The Identity and Function of Jews and Related Terms in the Fourth Gospel* (Ann Arbor, microfilm, 1972).

14. Von Wahlde cites Brown, 526, as holding this view, with 7:3 as an exception.

15. Von Wahlde, 174.

16. Ibid., 57.

17. Ibid., 47, n. 53.

18. His extended n. 136 on pp. 134–35 is important in this regard. Unlike most who look for a source behind the passion material, von Wahlde has no recourse to comparison with the Synoptics but uses his earlier criteria: "Pharisees" once, "chief priests" throughout, "Jews" as Judeans only, concept and place names in Aramaic and Greek in the two reverse orders, and no theological development beyond Jesus as "the Christ, the Son of God" (20:31).

19. D. Moody Smith, *Johannine Christianity: Essays on Its Setting, Sources, and Theology* (Columbia, 1984), 1–36.

20. These he had gone into in more detail in a paper of 1964, "The Sources of the Gospel of John," chapter 1.

21. Smith, *Johannine Christianity,* 16.

22. Ibid., 24; but see his earlier recording of resistance to the idea, p. 81.

23. "Divine man," a Hellenistic model that is a construct of twentieth-century scholarship and has been called into question as a reality of the ancient world on the confident terms with which it is employed in New Testament studies. Smith calls the existence "of such a christology in some sense native to Judaism," widely regarded as well established, "The Johannine Miracle Source" (1967), ibid., 65, 67.

24. Smith, *Johannine Christianity,* 35.

25. Smith, "The Sources," 60.

26. Ibid., 76.

27. *Catholic Biblical Quarterly* 51, 1 (1989): 147.

28. Wolfgang J. Bittner, *Jesu Zeichen in Johannesevangelium* (Tübingen, 1987).

29. J. Louis Martyn, *History and Theology in the Fourth Gospel* (New York, 1968); 2d rev. ed. (Nashville, 1979). See also some learned papers in reprint: *The Gospel of John in Recent History: Essays for Interpreters* (New York, 1978).

30. Martyn, "Glimpses into the History of the Johannine Community: From Its Origin through the Period of Its Life in Which the Fourth Gospel Was Composed," in Marinus de Jonge, ed., *L'Évangile de Jean: Sources, rédaction, théologie* (Gembloux and Leuven, 1977), 149–75.

31. Ibid., 158.

32. Ibid., 163.

33. Barnabas Lindars, *The Gospel of John* (London, 1972).

34. Lindars, *Behind the Fourth Gospel* (London, 1971).

35. Lindars, "Traditions behind the Fourth Gospel," in *L'Évangile de Jean,* ed. M. de Jonge, 107–24.

36. Ibid., 107.

37. Lindars, *Behind,* 47.

38. Oscar Cullmann, *The Johannine Circle* (London, 1976; German original, 1975), 9–10, 98.

39. John A. T. Robinson, *The Priority of John,* ed. J. F. Coakley (London, 1985).

40. Ibid., 5.

41. Ibid., 9.

42. Ibid., 20–21, quoting Kysar, 24.

43. Robinson, 67; elsewhere in a footnote he reports the unhappiness of A. J. B. Higgins and James Montgomery at calling it "the Fourth Gospel" (for the latter, a "scholastic affectation"), although Robinson employs the term throughout. See p. 4, n. 6.

44. Robinson, *Redating the New Testament* (London, 1976).

45. Robinson, *Priority,* 67, n. 150, summarizing his argument in ch. 9 of *Redating,* 254–311.

46. *TPOJ,* 23–24

47. See ibid., 24.

48. Ibid., 26.

49. Ibid.

50. Ibid., 8.

51. Ibid., 4.

52. Ibid., 5.

53. Review in *Journal of Biblical Literature* 108, 1 (1989): 156–58.

54. Cullmann, op. cit., 49.

55. See John Bowman, *The Fourth Gospel and the Jews* (Pittsburgh, 1975) for an explanation of this agricultural proverb (p. 114).

56. Cullmann, "Samaria and the Origins of the Christian Mission," in *The Early Church* (London, 1956). Barrett, op. cit., 243, n. 38, thinks the opinion wrong. See Raymond E. Brown, *The Community of the Beloved Disciple* (New York, 1979) for the suggestion that Jn 4 is a turning point in the Gospel for the "entrance into Johannine Christianity of another group which catalyzed the christological developments [viz., toward an increasingly 'higher' Johannine Christology]," p. 34. On Brown's *Community,* see further on pp. 85–86 below.

57. Alan Culpepper, *The Johannine School* (Missoula, 1974).

58. Ibid., 258–59.

59. Ibid., 287–89.

60. Ibid., 269.

61. Martin Hengel, *The Johannine Question* (Philadelphia, 1990).

62. Ibid., 130.

63. Ibid., 131.

64. Ibid., 103.

65. Ibid., 105; cf. 72–73.

66. See ibid., 114–19 with n. 52, p. 213. Besides the articles cited there, of P. Schäfer (*Judaica,* 1975), G. Stemberger (*Kairos,* 1977), R. Kimelman (*Journal of Theological Studies,* NS, 1982), and S. I. Katz (*Journal of Biblical Literature,* 1984), see Kimelman's shorter "*Birkat Ha-Minim* and the Lack of Evidence for an Anti-Christian Jewish Prayer in Late Antiquity," in E. P. Sanders et al., eds., *Jewish and Christian Self-Definition,* vol. 2, *Aspects of Judaism in the Greco-Roman Period* (Philadelphia, 1981), 226–44.

3. John as Religious Literature

1. Klaus Koch, *The Growth of the Biblical Tradition: The Form-Critical Method* (New York, 1969), 69.

2. Norman R. Petersen, *Literary Criticism for New Testament Critics* (Philadelphia, 1978). The first part of this short book is on

Mark's Gospel, the second, less successful part on a Lucan question. See also David Rhoads and Donald Michie, *Mark as Story: An Introduction to the Narrative of a Gospel* (Philadelphia, 1982).

3. Frank Kermode, *The Genesis of Secrecy: On the Interpretation of Narrative* (Cambridge, 1979); Northrop Frye, *The Great Code: The Bible and Literature* (New York and London, 1982) — prompting irreverent thoughts of a title such as *Shakespeare and Literature*.

4. David W. Wead, *The Literary Devices in John's Gospel* (1970).

5. R. Alan Culpepper, *Anatomy of the Fourth Gospel: A Study in Literary Design* (Philadelphia, 1983).

6. Jack Dean Kingsbury, *Matthew as Story* (Philadelphia, 1986).

7. Culpepper, 231.

8. Ibid., 232. Culpepper received some sharp criticism from Jeffrey Lloyd Staley in *The Print's First Kiss: A Rhetorical Investigation of the Implied Reader in the Fourth Gospel* (Atlanta, 1988) for his inaccurate use of terms such as *narrator, implied author,* and *implied reader* as if they were firmly fixed. The pun of Staley's title indicates that he is concerned with the impact made on the reader by a text prepared for oral delivery, but later captured first in manuscripts (a fluid medium), then print. That done, he examines the prologue followed by chs. 1–3 and five later passages where the narrator seems self-contradictory but has consciously planted tensions for the reader to embrace.

9. Culpepper, 234.

10. Ibid., 48–49.

11. Ibid., 35.

12. Ibid., 41.

13. Ibid., 43–48.

14. Ibid., 88.

15. Paul D. Duke, *Irony in the Fourth Gospel* (Atlanta, 1985), 147.

16. Ibid., 151.

17. Gail O'Day, *Revelation in the Fourth Gospel: Narrative Mode and Theological Claim* (Philadelphia, 1986).

18. Ibid., 26, quoting D. C. Muecke, "Irony Markers," *Poetics* 7 (1968): 365. O'Day cites favorably George W. MacRae, SJ, "Theology and Irony in the Fourth Gospel," in *The Word and the World: Essays in Honor of F. L. Moriarty,* ed. R. J. Clifford (Cambridge, 1973), 83–96.

19. O'Day, 113, citing Amos N. Wilder's *Theopoetic: Theology and the Religious Imagination* (Philadelphia, 1976), 92.

20. Ibid.

21. Godfrey C. Nicholson, *Death as Departure: The Johannine Descent-Ascent Schema* (Chico, 1983). Ernst Käsemann gave the Shaffer Lecture at Yale in 1966, published later that same year in German (Tübingen) but in English as *The Testament of Jesus: A Study of the Gospel of John in the Light of Chapter 17* (Philadelphia, 1968). He saw in this chapter the literary convention of the biblical address of a dying man, corresponding to the prologue and effectively bringing the Gospel to a close. It showed the whole Gospel to be a piece of "naïve docetism" in which the author "spiritualized old apocalyptic traditions." The church accepted into its canon through human error and God's providence this presentation of "Jesus as God walking the face of the earth" (p. 75), a "dangerous theology" that nonetheless "calls us into our creatureliness" and shows us "the one final testament of the earthly Jesus and his glory" (p. 78).

22. Nicholson, 166.

23. Marianne Meye Thompson, *The Humanity of Jesus in the Fourth Gospel* (Philadelphia, 1988).

24. Ibid., 128.

25. David Rensberger, *Johannine Faith and Liberating Community* (Philadelphia, 1988).

26. See ibid., 28–29.

27. Ibid., 60.

28. See ibid., 61.

29. In doing so he sides with Martyn, *History and Theology in the Fourth Gospel,* 2d ed., 87–88, but does not see in Nicodemus's anointing of Jesus' body (against Brown, Schnackenburg, and Lindars) a gesture of devotion, even confession (pp. 38–40). Jouette Bassler finds Jn leaving Nicodemus a completely ambiguous figure in the three places where he appears (3:1–21; 7:45–52; 19:38–42) as part of a cognitive "gap" intended by the author, forcing the reader to wrestle with the contours of Johannine faith. See Bassler, "Mixed Signals: Nicodemus in the Fourth Gospel," *Journal of Biblical Literature* 108, 4 (1989): 635–46.

30. See Rensberger, 74.

31. See ibid., 78–79, 110–11; cf. Frederick Herzog, *Liberation in the Light of the Fourth Gospel* (New York, 1972), which Rensberger thinks not without value, but, on balance, a disappointment because of its neglect of exegesis. A Salamanca dissertation that explores Jn

7:1–10:21 is Hugo C. Zorilla's *La fiesta de liberación de los oprimidos,* whose conclusions are summarized in *Mission Focus* 13 (1985): 21–24.

32. Rensberger, 114.

33. Wayne A. Meeks, "The Man from Heaven in Johannine Sectarianism," *Journal of Biblical Literature* 91 (1972): 44–72; cf. Marinus de Jonge, "Nicodemus and Jesus," in *Jesus: Stranger from Heaven and Son of God* (Missoula, 1974), 29–48, who sees Nicodemus's sympathy and incorrect faith in Jesus as set in opposition to Johannine faith.

34. Rensberger, 136f.

35. Jerome H. Neyrey, SJ, *An Ideology of Revolt: John's Christology in Social Science Perspective* (Philadelphia, 1988). For the remarks on point of view, see pp. 97 and 239, n. 8.

36. Ibid., 33.

37. Ibid.

38. Ibid., 35.

39. Ibid., 58.

40. Ibid., 92.

41. Ibid., 117–18; a fourth or final stage is "represented by ch. 21 and the moderation of earlier spiritualist tendencies (see 1 and 2 John as well)."

42. Ibid., 127.

43. Ibid., 147.

44. Raymond E. Brown, *The Community of the Beloved Disciple* (New York, 1979). See also D. Bruce Woll, *Johannine Christianity in Conflict: Authority, Rank, and Succession in the First Farewell Discourses* (Chico, 1989).

45. Raymond E. Brown, *The Epistles of John* (Garden City, 1982). A previous work on the longest of these was John Bogart's *Orthodox and Heretical Perfectionism in the Johannine Community as Evident in the First Epistle of John* (Missoula, 1977).

46. Bruce Malina, *The New Testament World: Insights from Cultural Anthropology* (Atlanta, 1981); later, *Christian Origins and Cultural Anthropology: Practical Models for Biblical Interpretation* (Atlanta, 1986). Douglas's first book-length presentation of group and grid was in *Natural Symbols* (New York, 1982).

47. Neyrey, 166.

48. Ibid., 143.

49. Ernst Käsemann, *The Testament of Jesus: A Study of the Gospel of John in the Light of Chapter 17* (Philadelphia, 1968).

50. Teresa Okure, RHCJ, *The Johannine Approach to Mission: A Contextual Study of John 4:1–42* (Tübingen, 1988).

51. Ibid., 50–51.

52. For the historical probabilities underlying the story of Jn 4, see ibid., 188–91.

53. Ibid., 187–88.

54. Gary M. Burge, *The Anointed Community: The Holy Spirit in the Johannine Tradition* (Grand Rapids, 1987).

55. Ibid., 41.

56. Felix Porsch, CSSp, *Pneuma und Wort: Ein exegetischer Beitrag zur Pneumatologie des Johannesevangeliums* (Frankfurt, 1974). Review by D. M. Smith, *Journal of Biblical Literature* 96, 3 (1977): 458–59. From this Gregorian University dissertation came a shorter study, *Anwalt der Glaubenden: Das Wirken des Geistes nach dem Zeugnis Johannesevangelium* (Stuttgart, 1978).

57. Ignace de la Potterie, SJ, *La vérité dans S. Jean,* 2 vols. (Rome, 1977). Burge refers particularly to his chapter 5, "Le Paraclet, l'Esprit de la vérité."

58. Burge, 43.

59. Ibid.

60. Ibid., 49.

61. See ibid., 81.

62. Ibid., 83, 84.

63. See ibid., 85, 87.

64. Ibid., 100.

65. See ibid., 148–49.

66. Ibid., 193.

67. Ibid., 220–21.

68. Severino Pancaro, *The Law in the Fourth Gospel: The Torah and the Gospel, Moses and Jesus, Judaism and Christianity according to John* (Leiden, 1975).

69. Ibid., 510–11.

70. Anthony Ernest Harvey, *Jesus on Trial: A Study in the Fourth Gospel* (London, 1976; Atlanta, 1977).

71. Ibid., 130.

72. See ibid., 131.

73. Ibid., 55.

74. See ibid., 5.

75. See ibid., 57.

76. J. Terence Forestell, CSB, *The Word of the Cross: Salvation as Revelation in the Fourth Gospel* (Rome, 1974).

77. Francis J. Moloney, SDB, *The Johannine Son of Man* (Rome, 1976).

78. Forestell, 16.

79. Barnabas Lindars, SSF, *Jesus Son of Man: A Fresh Examination of the Son of Man Sayings in the Gospels in the Light of Recent Research* (Grand Rapids, 1984). The quotation is on p. 155. Lindars agrees with Moloney that the use of Son of Man in 5:27 is titular and there it *may* be connected with Dan 7:13–14 — of which Jn should not be presumed ignorant. But even in that case it refers to the one whose crucifixion bespeaks God's glory. Interestingly, Lindars does not cite Forestell in his brief chapter on Jn (pp. 145–57) while largely coming to the same conclusion as he on what Son of Man means for this evangelist. Cf. Douglas R. A. Hare, *The Son of Man Tradition* (Minneapolis: Fortress, 1990), "John," pp. 79–111.

80. Birger Olsson, *Structure and Meaning in the Fourth Gospel: A Text-Lingusitic Analysis of John 2:1–11 and 4:1–42*, tr. J. Gray (Lund, 1974).

81. Raymond E. Brown, *The Epistles of John Translated with Introduction, Notes, and Commentary,* Anchor Bible 30 (Garden City, 1982). In 1973 there had appeared a translation of Rudolf Bultmann's *The Johannine Epistles* in the Hermeneia commentary (Philadelphia, 1973; Göttingen, 1967), and more recently Urban C. von Wahlde's *The Johannine Commandments: 1 John and the Struggle for the Johannine Tradition* (Mahwah, 1990). The latter builds on Brown to show that the opponents of 1 Jn in their interpretation of the Johannine commandments have one-sidedly exaggerated the role of the Spirit and underplayed that of Jesus.

82. Ed. L. Miller, *Salvation-History in the Prologue of John: The Significance of John 1:3/4* (Leiden: E. J. Brill, 1989).

83. James McCaffrey, *The House with Many Rooms: The Temple Theme of Jn 14:2–3* (Rome, 1988).

4. Treatments of Johannine Themes

1. Mark W. G. Stibbe, *The Gospel of John as Literature: An Anthology of Twentieth-Century Perspectives* (Leiden, 1993).

2. John Ashton, *The Interpretation of John,* 2d ed. (Edinburgh, 1997).

3. Ibid., 212.

4. R. Alan Culpepper and C. Clifton Black, eds., *Exploring the Gospel of John* (Louisville, 1996).

5. R. Alan Culpepper, *The Gospel and Letters of John* (Nashville, 1988).

6. D. Moody Smith, *The Theology of the Gospel of John* (Cambridge, 1995).

7. Ibid., 172.

8. Ibid.

9. Ibid., 174, n. 8.

10. Raymond F. Collins, *John and His Witness* (Collegeville, 1991).

11. Stanley B. Marrow, SJ, *The Gospel of John: A Reading* (Mahwah, 1995).

12. Andreas J. Köstenberger, *Encountering John: The Gospel in Historical, Literary, and Theological Perspective* (Grand Rapids, 1999).

13. Robert Kysar, *Preaching John* (Minneapolis, 2002).

14. Raymond F. Collins, *These Things Have Been Written: Studies on the Fourth Gospel* (Leuven, 1990).

15. *Books of the New Covenant* (in Hebrew; Israel: The United Bible Societies, 1976), translated by Joseph Atzmon, a Protestant, and Yohanan Elihai, a Catholic; sponsored by Melkite Greek Catholic Bishop Kaldani of Nazareth. Edition of 1996 has the word for "people" or "residents" at 9:22 and elsewhere, not *hayyehudim.*

16. Francis J. Moloney, SDB, *Belief in the Word: Reading John 1–4.* (Minneapolis, 1993); *Signs and Shadows: Reading John 5–12,* (Minneapolis, 1996); *Glory Not Dishonor: Reading John 13–21* (Minneapolis, 1998).

17. Xavier Léon-Dufour, *Lecture de l' Évangile selon Jean,* I, chapters 1–4 (1988); II, 5–12 (1990); III, 13–17 (1993); IV, 18–21 (1996) (Paris, Seuil).

18. Gail O'Day, "The Gospel of John," in *The New Interpreter's Bible* (Nashville, 1995), 9:493–865.

19. Charles H. Talbert, *Reading John* (New York, 1992).

20. Herman Ridderbos, *The Gospel of John: A Theological Commentary* (Grand Rapids, 1997).

21. Thomas L. Brodie, OP, *The Quest for the Origins of John's Gospel: A Source-Oriented Approach* (New York, 1993); *The Gospel according to John: A Literary and Theological Commentary* (New York, 1993).

22. Francis J. Moloney, SDB, *The Gospel according to John,* Sacra Pagina Series 4 (Collegeville, 1998).

23. Seán P. Kealy, CSSp, *John's Gospel and the History of Biblical Interpretation,* 2 vols. (Lewiston, N.Y., 2002).

24. Kenneth Grayston, *The Gospel of John* (Philadelphia, 1990).

25. Donald A. Carson, *The Gospel according to John* (Grand Rapids, 1991).

26. Ibid., 91.

27. R. Bieringer, D. Pollefeyt, and F. Vandecasteele-Vanneuville, eds., *Anti-Judaism and the Fourth Gospel: Papers of the Leuven Colloquium, 2000* (Assen, 2001).

28. Rudolph Schnackenburg, *The Johannine Epistles* (New York, 1992).

29. Georg Strecker, *The Johannine Epistles* (Minneapolis, 1996).

30. David Rensberger, *1 John, 2 John, 3 John* (Nashville, 1997).

31. Colin G. Kruse, *The Letters of John* (Grand Rapids, 2000).

32. William Loader, *The Johannine Epistles* (London, 1992).

33. Gerard S. Sloyan, *Walking in the Truth—Perseverers and Deserters: 1, 2, and 3 John* (Valley Forge, 1995).

34. Judith M. Lieu, *The Second and Third Epistles of John: History and Background* (Edinburgh, 1986).

35. Judith M. Lieu, *The Theology of the Johannine Epistles* (Cambridge, 1991).

36. Albert Denaux, ed., *John and the Synoptics* (Leuven, 1992).

37. Dwight Moody Smith, *John among the Gospels: The Relationship in Twentieth-Century Research* (Minneapolis, 1992).

38. M.-E. Boismard and Arnaud Lamouille, *L'Évangile de Jean: Synopse des Quatre Evangiles en français,* 3 vols. (Paris, 1972–77). See

now R. E. Brown, *An Introduction to the Gospel of John,* ed. F. J. Moloney (New York, 2003), 59–62.

39. Johannes Beutler, SJ, and Robert Fortna, eds., *The Shepherd Discourse of John 10 and Its Context* (New York, 1991).

40. Donald Senior, CP, *The Passion of Jesus in the Gospel of John* (Collegeville, 1991).

41. John Christopher Thomas, *Footwashing in John 13 and the Johannine Community* (Sheffield, 1991).

42. Fernando F. Segovia, *The Farewell of the Word: The Johannine Call to Abide* (Minneapolis, 1991).

43. Ibid., 58.

44. Anthony Tyrell Hanson, *The Prophetic Gospel: A Study of John and the Old Testament* (Edinburgh, 1991).

45. Ibid., 40.

46. Ibid., 63.

47. Ibid., 252.

48. Ibid., 49.

49. Margaret Davies, *Rhetoric and Reference in the Fourth Gospel* (Sheffield, 1992).

50. Adele Reinhartz, *The Word in the World: The Cosmological Tale in the Fourth Gospel* (Atlanta, 1992).

51. Ibid., 131.

52. Ibid., 93.

53. Jeffrey A. Trumbower, *Born from Above: The Anthropology of the Fourth Gospel* (Tübingen, 1992).

54. Ibid., 11.

55. Ibid., 13.

56. Ibid., 64.

57. Ibid., 69.

58. Udo Schnelle, *Antidocetic Christology in the Gospel of John: An Investigation of the Place of the Fourth Gospel in the Johannine School* (Minneapolis, 1992).

59. Ibid., 63.

60. Martin Scott, *Sophia and the Johannine Jesus* (Sheffield, 1992).

61. Ibid., 15.

62. Richard J. Cassidy, *John's Gospel in New Perspective: Christology and the Realities of Roman Power* (Maryknoll, 1992).

63. Joseph A. Grassi, *The Secret Identity of the Beloved Disciple* (Mahwah, 1992).

64. Mark W. G. Stibbe, *John as Storyteller: Narrative Criticism and the Fourth Gospel* (Cambridge, 1992); *John,* Readings: A New Biblical Commentary (Sheffield, 1993); *John's Gospel: New Testament Readings* (London, 1994).

65. Stibbe, *John as Storyteller,* 80–81.

66. John Painter, *The Quest for the Messiah: The History, Literature, and Theology of the Johannine Community,* 2d ed.; (Nashville, 1993).

67. Ibid., 119.

68. Ibid., 465–66.

69. Norman R. Petersen, *The Gospel of John and the Sociology of Light: Language and Characterization in the Fourth Gospel* (Valley Forge, 1993).

70. Ibid., 133.

71. J. Duncan M. Derrett, *The Victim: The Johannine Passion Narrative Reexamined* (Shipton-on-Stour, 1993).

72. Ibid., 9.

73. Ibid., 2.

74. Bruno Barnhart, *The Good Wine: Reading John from the Center* (Mahwah, 1993).

75. L. William Countryman, *The Mystical Way in the Fourth Gospel: Crossing Over into God* (Valley Forge, 1994).

76. R. Alan Culpepper, *John the Son of Zebedee: The Life of a Legend* (Columbia, S.C., 1994).

77. Dorothy Lee, *The Symbolic Narratives of the Fourth Gospel: The Interplay of Form and Meaning* (Sheffield, 1994).

78. James H. Charlesworth, *The Beloved Disciple: Whose Witness Validates the Gospel of John?* (Valley Forge, 1995).

79. Ibid., 422f.

80. Ibid., 431.

81. Craig R. Koester, *Symbolism in the Fourth Gospel: Meaning, Mystery, Community* (Minneapolis, 1995).

82. Ben Witherington III, *John's Wisdom: A Commentary on the Fourth Gospel* (Louisville, 1995).

83. David Mark Ball, *"I Am" in John's Gospel: Literary Function, Background, and Theological Implications* (Sheffield, 1996).

84. Ibid., 282.

85. Ibid.

86. Ibid.

87. Maurice Casey, *Is John's Gospel True?* (London, 1996).

88. Maarten J. J. Menken, *Old Testament Quotations in the Fourth Gospel: Studies in Textual Form* (Rampen, 1996).

89. Paul N. Anderson, *The Christology of the Fourth Gospel: Its Unity and Disunity in the Light of John 6* (Valley Forge, 1996).

90. Ibid., 112.

91. Ibid., 135.

92. Ibid., 166.

93. Ibid., 207–13.

94. Derek Tovey, *Narrative Art and Act in the Fourth Gospel* (Sheffield, 1997).

95. J. Massyngbaerde Ford, *Redeemer—Friend and Mother: Salvation in Antiquity and in the Gospel of John* (Fortress, 1997).

96. Jey J. Kanagaraj, *"Mysticism" in the Gospel of John: An Inquiry into Its Background* (Sheffield, 1998).

97. Bruce J. Malina and Richard L. Rohrbaugh, *Social-Science Commentary on the Gospel of John* (Minneapolis, 1998).

98. Ibid., 223.

99. Andrew T. Lincoln, *Truth on Trial: The Lawsuit Motif in the Fourth Gospel* (Peabody, 2000).

100. Ibid., 434.

101. Ibid., 473.

102. Tom Thatcher, *The Riddles of Jesus in John: A Study in Tradition and Folklore* (Atlanta, 2000).

103. Marianne Meye Thompson, *The God of the Gospel of John* (Grand Rapids, 2001).

104. Ibid., 6.

105. Ibid., 237–38.

106. Ford Larsson, *God in the Fourth Gospel: A Hermeneutical Study of the History of Interpretations* (Stockholm, 2001).

107. Mark A. Matson, *In Dialogue with Another Gospel? The Influence of the Fourth Gospel on the Passion Narrative of Luke* (Atlanta, 2001).

108. Demetrius R. Dumm, OSB, *A Mystical Portrait of Jesus: New Perspectives on John's Gospel* (Collegeville, 2001).

109. Sandra Schneiders, *Written That You May Believe: Encountering Jesus in the Fourth Gospel* (New York, 1999).

110. Ibid., 16.

111. Adele Reinhartz, *Befriending the Beloved Disciple: A Jewish Reading of the Gospel of John* (New York, 2001).

112. Ibid., 167.

113. Ibid., 141.

114. Ibid., 70.

115. François Vouga, *Le cadre historique et l'intention de Jean* (Paris, 1977).

116. Ibid., 110; so Dauer, 311.

117. John Ashton, *Understanding the Fourth Gospel* (Oxford, 1991).

118. Ibid., 151.

119. Ibid., 237.

120. Ibid.

121. Ibid., 405.

122. John Ashton, *Studying John: Approaches to the Fourth Gospel* (Oxford, 1994).

123. Ibid., 71.

124. Ibid., 86f.; *Dial.,* 60.

125. Ibid., 139.

126. Gunnar Østenstad, *Patterns of Redemption in the Fourth Gospel* (Lewiston, N.Y., 1998).

127. Adeline Fehribach, *The Women in the Life of the Bridegroom* (Collegeville, 1998).

128. Satoko Yamaguchi, *Women in the World of Jesus* (Maryknoll, 2002).

129. Fehribach, 175, n.

130. James L. Resseguie, *The Strange Gospel: Narrative Design and Point of View in John* (Brill, 2001).

131. Terry Griffith, *Keep Yourselves from Idols: A New Look at 1 John* (Sheffield, 2002).

132. Dorothy Lee, *Flesh and Glory: Symbol, Gender and Theology in the Gospel of John* (New York, 2002).

133.   Margaret M. Beirne, *Women and Men in the Fourth Gospel: A genuine Discipleship of Equals* (Sheffield, 2003).

134.   *The Johannine Corpus in the Early Church* (Oxford, 2004).

135.   Jane S. Webster, *Ingesting Jesus: Eating and Drinking in the Gospel of John* (Leiden, 2003).

136.   Mary L. Coloe, *God Dwells With Us: Temple Symbolism in the Fourth Gospel* (Collegeville, 2001).

Some Commentaries

Barrett, Charles Kingsley. *The Gospel according to St. John*. London: S.P.C.K., 1955; 2d rev. ed., Philadelphia: Westminster, 1978.

Beasley-Murray, George Raymond. *John*. Word Biblical Commentary 36. Waco: Word, 1987.

Becker, Jürgen. *Das Evangelium des Johannes*. 2 vols. Gütersloh: Gerd Mohn, 1979–81.

Bernard, John Henry. *The Gospel according to St. John*. 2 vols. New York: Scribner's, 1929.

Braun, François-Marie. *L'Évangile selon Saint Jean*. La Sainte Bible. Paris: Letouzey et Ané, 1946.

Brodie, Thomas L. *The Gospel according to John: A Literary and Theological Commentary*. New York: Oxford University Press, 1993.

Brown, Raymond Edward. *The Gospel according to John*. Anchor Bible 29 and 29A. Garden City: Doubleday, 1966–70.

_____. *The Epistles of John*. Anchor Bible 30. Garden City: Doubleday, 1982.

_____. *The Gospel and Epistles of John: A Concise Commentary*. Collegeville: Liturgical, 1988.

_____. *An Introduction to the Gospel of John*. Edited by Francis J. Moloney. New York: 2003.

Bultmann, Rudolf. *The Gospel of John*. Philadelphia: Westminster, 1971; German orig., Göttingen: Vandenhoeck und Ruprecht, 1941.

_____. *The Johannine Epistles*. Hermeneia. Philadelphia: Fortress, 1973; German orig., 1967.

Carson, D. A. *The Gospel according to John*. Grand Rapids: Eerdmans, 1991.

Ellis, Peter. *The Genius of John: A Composition Critical Commentary on the Fourth Gospel*. Collegeville: Liturgical, 1984.

Haenchen, Ernst. *John 1 and John 2*. Hermeneia. Philadelphia: Fortress, 1984; German orig., Tübingen: Siebeck (Mohr), 1980.

Hoskyns, Edwyn Clement, and Francis Noel Davey. *The Fourth Gospel*. London: Faber and Faber, 1940; 2d ed., 1947.

Kealy, Seán P. *John's Gospel and the History of Biblical Interpretation*. 2 vols. Lewiston, New York: Edwin Mellen, 2002.

Kieffer, René, "60. John." In John Barton, ed., *The Oxford Bible Commentary*, 960–1000. Oxford: Oxford University Press, 2001.

Keener, Craig S. *The Gospel of John: A Commentary*. 2 vols. Peabody: Hendrickson, 2003.

Léon-Dufour, SJ, Xavier. *Lecture de l'Évangile selon Jean,* I, chap. 1–4 (1988); II, 5–12 (1990); III, 13–17 (1993); IV, 18–21 (1996). Paris: Éditions du Seuil.

Lindars, SSF, Barnabas. *The Gospel of John*. New Century Bible. Grand Rapids: Eerdmans, 1972.

Moloney, SDB, Francis. *The Gospel of John*. Sacra Pagina Series 4. Collegeville: Liturgical, 1994. See also Ch.4, n.16, 3 vols., 1993-1998.

Morris, Leon. *The Gospel according to John*. The New International Critical Commentary. Rev. ed. Grand Rapids: Eerdmans, 1995.

O'Day, Gail R. "The Gospel of John." In *The New Interpreter's Bible,* 9:493–865. Nashville: Abingdon, 1995.

Perkins, Pheme. *The Gospel according to St. John: A Theological Commentary*. Chicago: Franciscan Herald, 1978.

_____. "John." In *The New Jerome Biblical Commentary,* 942–85. Englewood Cliffs: Prentice-Hall, 1989.

Rensberger, David. *1 John, 2 John, 3 John*. Nashville: Abingdon, 1997.

Ridderbos, Herman. *The Gospel of John: A Theological Commentary*. Grand Rapids: Eerdmans, 1997.

Schlatter, Adolf. *Der Evangelist Johannes*. 4th ed., Stuttgart: Calwer, 1975.

Schnackenburg, Rudolf. *The Gospel according to John*. 3 vols. New York: Crossroad, 1968–82; German orig., Freiburg: Herder, 1965–75.

_____, *The Johannine Epistles: Introduction and Commentary*. New York: Crossroad, 1992.

Sloyan, Gerard Stephen. *John*. Interpretation Series: A Biblical Commentary for Teaching and Preaching. Atlanta: John Knox, 1988.

_____, *Walking in the Truth—Perseverers and Deserters. The First, Second and Third Letters of John*. Valley Forge: Trinity Press International, 1995.

Smith, Dwight Moody, "John." In *Harper's Bible Commentary*, 1044–76. San Francisco: Harper and Row, 1988.

Talbert, Charles H. *Reading John: A Literary and Theological Commentary on the Fourth Gospel and the Johannine Epistles*. New York: Crossroad, 1992.

Witherington III, Ben. *John's Wisdom: A Commentary on the Fourth Gospel*. Louisville: Westminster John Knox, 1995.

Further Reading

Auerbach, Erich. *Mimesis: The Representation of Reality in Western Literature*. Princeton University Press, 1953.

Barrett, C. K. *The Gospel of John and Judaism*. Philadelphia: Westminster, 1975.

Bassler, Jouette. "The Galileans: A Neglected Factor in Johannine Community Research." *Catholic Biblical Quarterly* 43, 2 (April 1981): 243–57.

_____. "Mixed Signals: Nicodemus in the Fourth Gospel." *Journal of Biblical Literature* 108, 4 (Winter 1989): 635–46.

Belle, Gilbert van. *Johannine Bibliography, 1966–1985: A Cumulative and Classified Bibliography on the Fourth Gospel*. Leuven University Press, 1988.

Boer, Martinus C. de. *Johannine Perspectives on the Death of Jesus*. Kampen: Pharos, 1996.

Bowman, John. *The Fourth Gospel and the Jews*. Pittsburgh: Pickwick, 1975.

Braun, F.-M. *Jean le théologien et son évangile dans l'église ancienne*. 2 vols. Paris: J. Gabalda, 1959–64.

Brown, Raymond E. *The Community of the Beloved Disciple*. New York: Paulist, 1979.

Burge, Gary M. *The Anointed Community: The Holy Spirit in the Johannine Tradition*. Grand Rapids: Eerdmans, 1987.

Charlesworth, James H., ed. *John and the Dead Sea Scrolls*. 2d rev. ed. New York: Crossroad, 1990.

Cullmann, Oscar. *The Johannine Circle*. Philadelphia: Westminster, 1976; German orig., 1975.

_____. "Samaria and the Origins of the Christian Mission." In *The Early Church*. London: SCM, 1956.

Culpepper, R. Alan. *The Johannine School: An Investigation...Based on the Nature of the Ancient Schools*. Missoula: Scholars, 1975.

_____. *Anatomy of the Fourth Gospel: A Study in Literary Design*. Philadelphia: Fortress, 1983.

Dodd, C. H. *The Interpretation of the Fourth Gospel*. Cambridge: University Press, 1953.

_____. *Historical Tradition in the Fourth Gospel*. Cambridge: University Press, 1963.

Duke, Paul D. *Irony in the Fourth Gospel*. Atlanta: John Knox, 1985.

Ehrhardt, Arnold. *The Framework of the New Testament Stories*. Cambridge: Harvard University Press, 1964.

Eusebius. *The Ecclesiastical History*. Translated by Kirsopp Lake. 2 vols. Cambridge: Harvard University Press, 1926–1932); *The History of the Church from Christ to Constantine*. Translated by G. A. Williamson. Harmondsworth: Penguin, 1965.

Faure, Alexander. "Die alttestamentlichen Zitate im 4. Evangelium und die Quellenscheidungshypothese." *Zeitschrift für die neutestamentliche Wissenschaft* 21 (1922): 99–121.

Forestell, J. Terence. *The Word of the Cross: Salvation as Revelation in the Fourth Gospel*. Rome: Pontifical Biblical Institute, 1974.

Fortna, Robert T. *The Gospel of Signs: A Reconstruction of the Narrative Source Underlying the Fourth Gospel*. New York and London: Cambridge University Press, 1970.

_____. *The Fourth Gospel and Its Predecessor: From Narrative Source to Present Gospel*. Philadelphia: Fortress, 1988.

Glasson, Thomas F. *Moses in the Fourth Gospel*. Naperville: A.R. Allenson, 1963.

Harrington, SJ, Daniel. *John's Thought and Theology: An Introduction*. Wilmington: Michael Glazier, 1990.

Harvey, A. E. *Jesus on Trial: A Study in the Fourth Gospel*. Atlanta: John Knox, 1977.

Herzog, Frederick. *Liberation Theology: Liberation in the Light of the Fourth Gospel*. New York: Seabury, 1972.

Howard, W. F. *The Fourth Gospel in Recent Criticism and Interpreta-tion*. Revised by C. K. Barrett. London: Epworth, 1955.

Jonge, Marinus de, ed. *L' Évangile de Jean: Sources, rédaction, théolo-gie*. Gembloux: Duculot; Leuven: University Press, 1977.

_____. *Jesus: Stranger from Heaven and Son of God*. Missoula: Schol-ars, 1977.

Karris, Robert. *Jesus and the Marginalized in John's Gospel*. Col-legeville: Michael Glazier/Liturgical, 1990.

Käsemann, Ernst. *The Testament of Jesus: A Study of the Gospel of John in the Light of Chapter 17*. Philadelphia: Fortress, 1968; German orig., 1966.

Katz, Steven T. "Issues in the Separation of Judaism and Christianity after 70 C.E.: A Reconsideration." *Journal of Biblical Literature* 103, 1 (1984): 43–76.

Kermode, Frank. *The Genesis of Secrecy: On the Interpretation of Nar-rative*. Cambridge: Harvard University Press, 1979.

Kiley, Mark. "The Exegesis of God: Jesus' Signs in John 1–11." In *SBL Seminar Papers,* 555–69. Atlanta: Scholars, 1988.

Kimelman, Reuven. "*Birkat Ha-Minim* and the Lack of Evidence for a Jewish Anti-Christian Prayer in Late Antiquity." In E. P. Sanders et al., eds., *Jewish and Christian Self-Definition,* vol. 2, *Aspects of Judaism in the Greco-Roman Period,* 226–44. Philadelphia: Fortress, 1981.

Kurz, SJ, William S. *The Farewell Addresses in the New Testament*. Wilmington: Michael Glazier, 1990.

Kysar, Robert. *The Fourth Evangelist and His Gospel*. Minneapolis: Augsburg, 1975.

_____. *John: The Maverick Gospel*. Atlanta: John Knox, 1976.

_____. "The Gospel of John in Current Research." *Religious Studies Review* 9, 4 (1983): 314–23.

_____. *John's Story of Jesus*. Philadelphia: Fortress, 1984.

_____. "The Fourth Gospel: A Report on Recent Research." In H. Tem-porini and W. Haase, eds., *Aufstieg und Niedergang der Römis-cher Welt,* II/3, 2389–2480. Berlin: de Gruyter, 1985.

Lindars, SSF, Barnabas. *Jesus Son of Man: A Fresh Examination of the Son of Man Sayings in the Gospels*. Grand Rapids: Eerdmans, 1984.

MacRae, SJ, George W. "Theology and Irony in the Fourth Gospel." In R. J. Clifford, *The Word and the World*. Cambridge, Mass.: Weston College, 1973.

_____. "The Fourth Gospel and Religionsgeschichte." *Catholic Biblical Quarterly* 32, 1 (1970): 13–24.

Malatesta, SJ, Edward. *St. John's Gospel: 1920–1965*. Rome: Pontifical Biblical Institute, 1967.

Malina, Bruce. *The New Testament World: Insights from Cultural Anthropology*. Atlanta: John Knox, 1981.

_____. *Christian Origins and Cultural Anthropology*. Atlanta: John Knox, 1986.

Martyn, J. Louis. *History and Theology in the Fourth Gospel*. 2d rev. ed. Nashville: Abingdon, 1979.

_____. "Glimpses into the History of the Johannine Community." In Marinus de Jonge, ed., *L' Évangile de Jean: Sources, rédaction, théologie*. Gembloux: Duculot/Leuven: University Press, 1977.

_____. *The Gospel of John in Recent History*. New York: Paulist, 1978.

Meeks, Wayne A. *The Prophet-King: Moses Traditions and the Johannine Christology*. Leiden: E. J. Brill, 1967.

_____. "The Man from Heaven in Johannine Sectarianism." *Journal of Biblical Literature* 91 (1972): 44–72.

Metzger, Bruce. *The Canon of the New Testament: Its Origin, Development, and Significance*. Oxford: Clarendon, 1987.

Moloney, SDB, Francis. *The Johannine Son of Man*. 2d ed. Rome: Ateneo Salesiano, 1979.

Morris, Leon. *Jesus Is the Christ: Studies in the Theology of John*. Grand Rapids: Eerdmans, 1971.

Neyrey, SJ, Jerome. *An Ideology of Revolt: John's Christology in Social Science Perspective*. Philadelphia: Fortress, 1988.

Nicholson, Godfrey C. *Death as Departure: The Johannine Descent-Ascent Schema*. Chico: Scholars, 1983.

Nicol, W. *The Sēmeia in the Fourth Gospel: Tradition and Redaction*. Leiden: Brill, 1972.

O'Day, Gail. *Revelation in the Fourth Gospel: Narrative, Mode, and Theological Claim*. Philadelphia: Fortress, 1986.

Okure, RHCJ, Teresa. *The Johannine Approach to Mission: A Contextual Study of John 4:1–42*. Tübingen: Mohr (Siebeck), 1988.

Olsson, Birger. *Structure and Meaning in the Fourth Gospel: A Text-Linguistic Analysis of John 2:1–11 and 4:1–42.* Lund: Gleerup, 1974.

Pagels, Elaine. *The Johannine Gospel in Gnostic Exegesis: Heracleon's Commentary on John.* Missoula: Scholars, 1973.

Pancaro, Severino. *The Law in the Fourth Gospel: The Torah and the Gospel, Moses and Jesus, Judaism and Christianity according to John.* Leiden: Brill, 1975.

Petersen, Norman R. *Literary Criticism for New Testament Critics.* Philadelphia: Fortress, 1978.

Porsch, CSSp, Felix. *Pneuma und Wort: Ein exegetische Beitrag zur Pneumatologie des Johannesevangeliums.* Frankfurt: Josef Knecht, 1974.

Potterie, SJ, I. de la. *La vérité dans S. Jean.* 2 vols. Rome: Pontifical Biblical Institute, 1977.

_____. *The Hour of Jesus: The Passion and the Resurrection of Jesus according to John.* New York: Alba House, 1989.

Reinhartz, Adele. *Befriending the Beloved Disciple: A Jewish Reading of the Gospel of John.* New York: Continuum, 2001.

Rensberger, David. *Johannine Faith and Liberating Community.* Philadelphia: Westminster, 1988.

Richter, Georg. *Studien zum Johannesevangelium.* Edited by Josef Hainz. Regensburg: Friedrich Pustet, 1977.

Robinson, John A. T. *The Priority of John.* Edited by J. F. Coakley. London: SCM, 1985.

Ruckstuhl, Eugen. *Die literarische Einheit des Johannesevangeliums.* Freiburg/Switz.: Paulus, 1951.

Sanders, E. P., et al., eds. *Jewish and Christian Self-Definition,* vol. 2, *Aspects of Judaism in the Greco-Roman Period.* Philadelphia: Fortress, 1981.

Schein, Bruce E. *Following in the Way: The Setting of John's Gospel.* Minneapolis: Augsburg, 1980.

Schweizer, Eduard. *Egō Eimi: Die religionsgeschictliche Herkunft...der johanneischen Bildreden.* 2d ed. Göttingen: Vandenhoeck und Ruprecht, 1965.

Segovia, Fernando F. *Love Relationships in the Fourth Gospel.* Atlanta: John Knox, 1982.

_____. *The Farewell of the Word: The Johannine Call to Abide*. Minneapolis: Fortress, 1991.

Smalley, Stephen. *John: Evangelist and Interpreter*. Greenwood: Attic, 1978.

Smith, D. Moody. *The Composition and Order of the Fourth Gospel: Bultmann's Literary Theory*. New Haven: Yale University Press, 1965.

_____. *Johannine Christianity: Essays on Its Setting, Sources, and Theology*. Columbia: University of South Carolina Press, 1984.

Thompson, Marianne Meye. *The Humanity of Jesus in the Fourth Gospel*. Philadelphia: Fortress, 1988.

_____. *The Incarnate Word: Perspectives on Jesus in the Fourth Gospel*. Peabody: Hendrickson, 1993.

Thyen, Hartwig. "Aus der Literatur zum Johannesevangelium." *Theologische Rundschau* 39 (1974) and 42 (1977).

Von Wahlde, Urban C. *The Earliest Version of John's Gospel: Recovering the Gospel of Signs*. Wilmington: Michael Glazier, 1989.

_____. *The Johannine Commandments: 1 John and the Struggle for the Johannine Tradition*. Mahwah: Paulist, 1990.

Vouga, François. "The Johannine School: A Gnostic Tradition in Primitive Christianity." *Biblica* 69 (1988): 371–85.

_____. *Le cadre historique et l'intention de Jean*. Paris, 1977.

Wijngaards, John. *The Gospel of John and His Letters*. Message of Biblical Spirituality 10. Wilmington: Michael Glazier, 1986.

Wilder, Amos N. *Theopoetic: Theology and the Religious Imagination*. Philadelphia: Westminster, 1976.

Woll, Bruce. *Johannine Christianity in Conflict: Authority, Rank, and Succession in the First Farewell Discourse*. Chico: Scholars, 1981.

Yee, Gale A. *Jewish Feasts and the Gospel of John*. Wilmington: Michael Glazier, 1989.

Author Index

Subject Index

Scripture Index

Other Books in This Series

Other Books in This Series

What are they saying about Catholic Ethical Method?
  by Todd A. Salzman

What are they saying about New Testament Apocalyptic?
  by Scott M. Lewis, S.J.

What are they saying about Environmental Theology?
  by John Hart

What are they saying about the Catholic Epistles?
  by Philip B. Harner

What are they saying about Theological Method?
  by J. J. Mueller, S.J.

What are they saying about Mark?
  by Daniel J. Harrington, S.J.

What are they saying about The Letter to the Hebrews?
  by Daniel J. Harrington, S.J.